# GOOD COP BAD COP

Police Misconduct and Corruption

**Kevin Moore**

Published by Saron Publishers in 2021



ISBN-13: 978-1-913297-16-9

Saron Publishers
Pwllmeyrick House
Mamhilad
Mon
NP4 8RG

www.saronpublishers.co.uk

info@saronpublishers.co.uk

Follow us on Facebook and Twitter

Cover design by © Tassam Designs 2021

# DEDICATION

For Ann

By the same author

My Way
Real Life Murder Investigations

Proceeds from the sale of this book will go to the police charity known as Care of Police Survivors (COPS).

COPS is a UK charity dedicated to helping the families of police officers and police staff who have lost their lives on duty to rebuild their lives. They aim to ensure that surviving family members have the help they need to cope with such tragedy and they remain part of the police family.

# CONTENTS

# FOREWORD

Corruption and misconduct within the police service have a considerable negative impact on public trust and confidence. Traditionally, the police have scored highly when measured against others such as teachers, doctors, solicitors and politicians, in terms of trustworthiness. Therefore, failures in this regard can have a devastating impact on the maintenance of law and order in its totality, if taken to the extreme. Is it a case of a 'few bad apples' or is the problem much wider than that?

There have been many causes célèbres over the years, where the conduct of police officers has fallen short of public expectations. Police corruption and misconduct can show itself in many ways, from taking bribes from top-end criminals at one end, through so-called 'noble cause' corruption and on to minor indiscretions at the other. However, even the latter can lead to worsening behaviour, negatively affecting whole teams of police officers. Such things can eat away at an organisation like a cancer.

What I have set out to do in this book is describe the different forms of corruption and what they mean in reality. I have tried to unpick the potential impact of police culture on corruption and assess the effectiveness of measures in place to overcome misdemeanors committed by officers. Additionally, I have tried to describe the changes that have taken place during the history of the police to overcome misconduct.

To outline what corruption looks like in practice, I have used cases of corruption and alleged corruption as examples. I hope these are both interesting and thought-provoking.

I also focus on the potential minefield for policing in terms of both handling informants and undercover policing. These areas provide probably the greatest risk for the service and therefore it is right that, recently, changes have been made to procedures to bring about greater transparency and scrutiny.

Finally, I refer to current trends regarding police misconduct and corruption and discuss what the future may hold.

My personal view is simple. The vast majority of serving police officers do a fine job – honest, hard-working and doing their best to protect the public. Policing is unique. It places officers in positions where it is inevitable that their moral compasses will be severely tested. I don't necessarily mean they are susceptible to 'going native' because most do a great job. However, in doing that job, the public expects officers to push the boundaries in order to uphold the rule of law and do right by them. This inevitably means that officers are expected to be 'lawfully audacious'. At times, there is an exceptionally fine dividing line.

The following quote best sums up this subject:

> It is my belief that most police officers are good hard working public servants... most police forces place their reputation above the law and the people they serve. The police have a totally unique place in Society, they are operationally independent.
>
> The police swear an oath to uphold the Law and to investigate crimes without fear or favour; it is this oath that separates them from the Public... the police literally can and have got away with murder, this often happens whilst some officers look the other way. When the police misbehave, they render the oath and office of constable...meaningless.

*(Ian Puddick - a former management consultant. He has advised Buckingham Palace HM the Queen Communications, CEO Communications Rolls Royce and Vodafone and recently advised the Cabinet Office re crisis communication. Ian now manages a Leak Detection Company based in London.)*

I could not have put the case better myself!

# CHAPTER 1

## What constitutes police misconduct and corruption?

The public often sees policing as the most trustworthy of all occupations. Public attitude surveys conducted over the years regularly place them above the legal profession, teachers and even doctors. So expectations are extremely high and police misconduct and corruption fascinates both the public and academics. Just consider the massive viewing figures for the former TV series *Between the Lines* and more recently *Line of Duty*, with the latter about to enter its sixth series.

So why is this and is this trust misplaced? Fortunately, instances of serious misconduct or corruption within the police are relatively few which probably accounts for the huge amounts of publicity which such events attract.

A phrase that has often been used to describe the police since their inception has been 'the police are the public and the public are the police'. Another oft-used description is that 'they are ordinary human beings doing an extraordinary job'. Presumably, this means they are as susceptible to the same human failings as the rest of society?

My view of things, having served as a police officer for over thirty-one years and worked for the police for almost forty years, is this. Police officers are indeed ordinary people. Like others, we have feelings, beliefs and needs. What sets police officers apart is the fact that they wish to serve and protect the public. Where others may be tempted to look the other way and maybe commit wrongs themselves, most police officers will recognise wrongs but possess the moral courage to say, 'No, that is wrong and I will never do that.'

However, the fact remains that there have been, and always will be, those police officers who 'go the wrong way'. The most important thing, therefore, is to ensure two things. Firstly, selection processes, such as vetting systems, must be as rigorous as possible. Secondly, mechanisms need to be in place to ensure that the police themselves are 'policed'. Both areas are critical and will be explored more fully later.

Another term often referred to when considering police corruption involves talking about 'a few bad apples'. When corruption is found, every organisation, including the police service, tends to suggest that the problem is confined to a few rogue members or 'bad apples'. This view of corruption and misconduct, whilst certainly more palatable, needs to be considered in greater depth.

Whilst it is perfectly possible for an individual or group to engage in highly unethical conduct, the history of policing has too many examples of institutionalised corruption for this explanation to carry much credence. Moreover, the notion of 'bad apples' has a number of far-reaching and potentially damaging implications. First, it narrows the scope of attention, directing concern away from others, often those in positions of authority, whose conduct also ought to be subject to scrutiny. Second, it implies that, barring the individual 'bad apple', everything in the organisation is otherwise sound. This is rarely the case and cannot be assumed. Third, and linked to this earlier point, the very notion of 'bad apples' implies little is required other than the investigation and punishment of these individuals.

Punishment, often severe, of a small number of individuals therefore becomes the default response to a corruption scandal. Such a response is flawed in at least two ways. It assumes that such punishments will 'send a message' to other officers about expected standards of conduct. This may have some substance but the evidence for any deterrent effect is not strong. Worse still, as suggested, such an approach fails to identify all those likely to be implicated in the wrongdoing. Often there is a failure to hold supervisors or managers to account, for example. Also, it fails to confront the structural problems that underpin the misconduct at the centre of the scandal. Indeed, there is little that could be more damaging to the health of the police service than simply using a 'bad apples' explanation in response to corruption. The impact of wrongdoing in the police service is considerable for all of us. There are many examples internationally of police forces being held in total contempt by not only their own citizens but many others, because corruption within their organisations is rife.

Policing has always relied on discipline within the organisation, albeit the levels of discipline are far less now than they used to be. The lower the levels of discipline within the service, the higher the risks of officers being involved in misconduct.

Just the same as anybody else, police officers are subject to the criminal law. So, any officer alleged to have been involved in criminal conduct is investigated in just the same way as any other citizen. Who conducts such investigations will be determined at the outset when evidence first becomes available to suggest that an officer may be guilty of a criminal offence. The matter can be investigated by independent officers from the suspected officer's own force or from another force, agreed in consultation with what is now the Independent Office for Police Conduct (IOPC). Indeed, the IOPC can conduct investigations in its own right.

Historically, the service has also always been subject to regulations to lay down what is expected of those serving and what the ramifications are likely to be if officers fail to comply. Individual officers were and still are responsible and are held accountable for their actions. However, regulations were not formally laid down until the 1960s. More recently, these have moved towards a more ethical position, and similarly the language has moved from discipline to misconduct. This subtle change is shown in the fact that the regulations were known as 'discipline regulations', whereas they are now known as 'conduct regulations'. This, it has been argued, was to move away from punishment towards a more conciliatory tone, with lessons being learned and things being put right. Ultimately, if a case is made out, officers potentially continue to face a hearing and punishment if cases are proven.

There has always been a healthy scepticism within the mindsets of most officers. There was an oft-used phrase which goes something like, 'The job would be brilliant if it weren't for the public.' Such phraseology contained a large slice of irony but there is some truth in it. Police officers often feel they are up against everyone on occasions. There is arguably almost a siege mentality, especially when there is open criticism in the media or in political circles, and an 'us and them' attitude develops as a result. This is really important when considering why some officers become corrupt. I have seen how officers can, sometimes, lose their focus and their reasons for joining in the first place, should this level of cynicism get out of control. Personal values can become affected as a result. Put another way, it reminds me of the football chant of Millwall fans who often sing, *We are Millwall from the Den, no one likes us but we don't care!* (sung to the tune of Rod Stewart's *Sailing*). My point therefore is simply this. Officers who develop this type of attitude could become more susceptible to corruption as they cease to care anymore. Thankfully, the vast majority retain the dark humour and the healthy cynicism and continue to do a great job.

From the very earliest days, from the advent of the original police service by Sir Robert Peel in 1839, police officers were rightly subjected to strict conditions as servants of the Crown, rather than traditional employees. However, these would be seen as archaic now. Indeed, a quick look at the earliest conditions makes one wonder why anyone would become a constable!

Before attending for the medical and interview to join the police, they were advised to have a bath! Working hours consisted of eight-, ten- or twelve-hour shifts, seven days a week. Officers were expected to walk around twenty miles a shift. There was no allowance for breaks, but officers could store a snack in their top hats and eat whilst on duty. No rest days, and only one week's unpaid holiday each year. Police officers were encouraged to grow beards as shaving was regarded as unhealthy, but beards were not to exceed two inches in length. Officers were not allowed to vote in elections. Whereas, in later years, it was believed essential to build relationships with the public, at first amazingly, they were warned to expect a hostile reception and should be prepared to be assaulted, stabbed or stoned. Officers could not 'gossip' with the public and should not converse even with colleagues, except to exchange a word and move on. The superintendent had to be informed before constables could associate, eat or drink with civilians. They were not allowed to sit down in public houses at any time and had to wear their uniform at all times to prevent accusations of spying on the public - a duty band was worn to show that he was on duty. Why did anyone join, especially as their private lives were restricted to such an extent?

Similarly, the creation of the police force suffered from a lack of support, not only amongst the public themselves but also within political circles and the so-called higher classes. Right from the outset, it seems there was an in-built distrust of the police, even from those who created them! All of which helps to explain elements that are prevalent within the organisation now and have been, right from the beginning.

It is important at this point to consider some history as regards police corruption. From the earliest days of the Bow Street Runners, through the formation of the New Police in the 1820s, to the phone-hacking scandal of recent times, policing in the United Kingdom has been punctuated with examples of malpractice and misconduct. The range of corrupt activities uncovered has included concealing serious crimes, bribery, fabricating and planting evidence, and committing serious crimes including allegations of murder.

Of course, sometimes corruption is all about plain and simple greed!

In 1957, the then Brighton Borough Police Force made the news for all the wrong reasons in what became one of the most infamous police corruption cases in history. On 2 October, at a press conference in Brighton Town Hall, Chief Constable Charles Ridge *(below)* announced he had asked Scotland Yard to investigate 'certain allegations of irregularities' in the force.

Three weeks later, Ridge himself was arrested, along with Detective Inspector John Hammersley, Detective Sergeant Trevor Heath and two members of the public, Anthony Lyons and Samuel Bellson, and all were charged with a variety of corrupt practices. Their trial lasted three weeks, with the prosecution case centring on a group of witnesses who were prepared to admit to criminal activities and illegal dealings with the accused officers.

## GOOD COP BAD COP

Alan Bennett, a company director, had been a known criminal since 1949 and had served ten prison sentences before coming to Brighton as a chef, opening the Astor Club in 1954, better known as the Bucket of Blood. Despite the club's reputation for violence and criminal activity, it was never raided by the police, a fact that became the basis of the prosecution case. Another witness, Alice Brabiner, claimed in court that she had taken part in an illegal abortion and that Heath had been paid £68 to 'do what he could to help me', in other words, to make the whole thing go away. Ernest Waite, a greengrocer, who admitted to dealing in stolen property, claimed he had a 'gentleman's agreement' with Hammersley whereby, for £200, Waite agreed not to trade in Brighton, but was given a free hand outside the town. Various other witnesses also gave evidence, most of them having criminal convictions, and all stated that their dealings had been accompanied by financial payments.

However, some officers also gave evidence for the prosecution. PC Frank Knight told the court that he had turned down an offer of cash from Heath, who had asked Knight if he wanted to earn £10 a week, adding, 'It's all right, your job won't fall flat.' After Knight said he was not interested, Heath stated that it did not bother him, even though he was to be given £5 for setting it up, as he had other illegal financial benefits.

Detective Constable Ray Hovey also gave evidence for the prosecution. Asked why he did not report his suspicions to Chief Constable Ridge, he stated that to have done so would have had a detrimental effect on his career, as the Chief Constable held Heath in high regard.

After the jury heard details of their excellent police records and commendations, Hammersley and Heath were both found guilty and sentenced to five years' imprisonment. In sentencing, the Judge commented that, as Ridge had not given them the professional and moral leadership to which they were entitled, their sentences were less harsh than they might have been.

Although the officers had acted with the support of Ridge, the prosecution found it impossible to substantiate the charges against him. Testimonies from subordinate officers were not sufficient to obtain a conviction against a Chief Constable in the 1950s, so Ridge was eventually acquitted, unlike his subordinates, but in a scathing statement before allowing Ridge to leave the dock, the judge remarked that the conspiracy might in future be used in Brighton to discredit officers and their evidence. Therefore, the force had to have a new leader, one 'who will be a new influence and who will set a different example from that which has lately obtained'. A damning acquittal.

The Royal Commission on the Police, established by RA Butler in 1960 under the chairmanship of Sir Henry Willink, was prompted in part by such cases of alleged or actual misconduct. Despite it giving British policing a glowing endorsement, allegations of corruption emerged shortly after its final report.

As the Police Bill (subsequently the Police Act 1964) was passing through Parliament, the local press, and later the national newspapers, began to print allegations concerning brutality by officers in Sheffield. The case led to the termination of the careers, not just of the officers from the Crime Squad accused of assaulting witnesses, but also of senior officers.

In a pattern that has subsequently become well established in corruption literature, the force's initial reaction to the allegations was to attempt to cover them up, and, in the highest echelons, to act to minimise the impact on the force. In a move prompted and supported by the Home Office, the Chief Constable and the Senior Investigating Officer (a chief superintendent) were subsequently suspended, pending an inquiry by the Watch Committee, (later the Police Authority), who oversaw forces. A short time later, the Chief Constable resigned as did the detective chief superintendent, both, in effect, jumping before they were pushed.

A second case, which also emerged in mid-1963 and involved allegations of police brutality, concerned a detective sergeant in the Metropolitan Police, named Harold Challenor. The case came to light after a series of arrests made by Challenor and others at a protest demo during a royal state visit. Challenor, it was shown in court, had planted evidence on a few suspects, (the evidence being half bricks), not only in this case but in a series of others. What was equally disturbing was the discovery that Challenor was suffering from quite serious mental ill health but had been allowed to carry on with his duties. This was another case, not just of serious misconduct, but a failure of line management. Interestingly, given what was to surface in the Metropolitan Police later in the decade, one of the recommendations from an inquiry set up to look into the Challenor affair was that there should be greater integration of CID and the uniformed branch, together with much greater attention to record keeping and evidence handling.

In the space of fewer than ten years, at least four separate corruption scandals involving Metropolitan Police officers were uncovered. It all began with journalists from *The Times* tape-recording conversations between detectives and criminals, in which covering up serious crimes was discussed. Equally shocking to many was the apparent inability of those investigating the abuses to bring anyone to justice. Other scandals emerged, in particular concerning the Drug Squad and the Obscene Publications Squad. There were even allegations, toward the end of the 1970s, that detectives had been involved in major armed robberies. Even the appointment of a reformist Commissioner, Sir Robert Mark, failed to break the cycle of scandal followed by failed investigation. The huge and heralded Operation Countryman, established by Mark's successor, Sir David McNee, petered out in an unseemly exchange of allegations and counter-allegations of malpractice, incompetence and corruption.

The criminal misconduct highlighted in the late 1960s and 1970s was closely followed by a series of miscarriages of justice, uncovered mainly in the 1980s, in which a range of abuses, including suppressing evidence, beating suspects, tampering with confessional evidence and perjury, were found to have occurred. An earlier case involving the murder of Maxwell Confait, and the subsequent overturning of the convictions of two men found guilty based on their confessions, led more or less directly to the establishment of the Royal Commission on Criminal Procedure and then, to the passage of the Police and Criminal Evidence Act

*Sir David McNee*

1984. The cases uncovered during the 1980s, ie the Birmingham Six, the Guildford Four, the Carl Bridgewater affair, and the activities of the West Midlands Serious Crime Squad, involved activities often misleadingly referred to as 'noble cause' corruption. Such corruption is, as the literature on the subject suggests, something which is an ever-present issue for the police service, as illustrated by the range and plentiful nature of allegations that have arisen since the major miscarriages of justice in the 1970s and 1980s. The cases, some infamous and others less so, included a number of allegations. There were claims of thirteen cover-ups and other corruption in relation to the Brinks Mat robbery, and impropriety suggestions in the Stephen Lawrence murder investigation. Suggestions of inappropriate relationships with news organisations, including the sale of information and alleged undermining of investigations in the phone-hacking scandal, were well-documented. Historically, allegations were made regarding the misuse of the 'super grass' system, including the manufacture of evidence, and damaging allegations regarding the deliberate promotion of misinformation in relation to the shooting of Jean Charles de Menezes. Suggestions of possible impropriety were linked to both the murder of private investigator Daniel Morgan in south east London in 1987, while he was looking into allegations of police corruption, and also to the subsequent investigation. Most recently, there were allegations of significant misconduct, including criminal activity and perjury, by undercover members of the Special Demonstration Squad.

The various discipline codes and regulations that govern the actions of police officers have changed over the years. The Police Act of 1964 was the first major attempt to bring about formal regulations. To begin with, this outlined the responsibilities of Chief Constables:

> The chief officer of police for any police area shall be liable in respect of torts committed by constables under his direction and control in the performance or purported performance of their functions in like manner as a master is liable in respect of torts committed by his servants in the course of their employment, and accordingly shall in respect of any such tort be treated for all purposes as a joint tort feasor.

In other words, Chief Constables were responsible for the actions of their officers.

It then identifies the responsibilities of forces and their Police Authorities to meet the costs of damages in cases brought against the Chief Constable and officers and states that these will be met from the police fund.

It goes on to discuss the investigation of complaints against police officers. It states that Chief Constables must record complaints from the public, made against officers within the force. These complaints must be subject to investigation and, if the Home Office deems it serious enough, Chief Constables must request the complaint is investigated by another force. It also makes clear that, if the matter involves potential criminal conduct, a report, following an initial investigation, should be sent to the Director of Public Prosecutions (DPP) to see if criminal charges should be brought. The Act also refers to the responsibilities of Police Authorities to oversee the way in which their forces record and investigate complaints. In Sussex, for example, a sub-group of the Police Authority used to meet regularly with senior management from the Discipline and Complaints department and physically look at a sample of ongoing complaint investigations.

The Police Discipline Regulations, in place from the 1960s, remained pretty much untouched until more recent times. This Discipline Code consisted of several offences. Firstly, *discreditable conduct* was an offence committed when 'a member of a police force acted in a disorderly manner or any manner prejudicial to discipline or reasonably likely to bring discredit on the reputation of the force or of the police service'.

It's immediately obvious that the language used is convoluted and long-winded. To save endless repetition of the same phrases, the other offences will be summarised.

The second matter involved *misconduct towards a member of a police force*. Here, an offence occurred when the conduct of a member of a force towards another member could be described as oppressive or abusive. In the most extreme cases, it could be where a member of a police force assaulted another member.

An offence of *disobedience to orders* took place if a member of a police force, without sufficient reason, disobeyed or neglected to carry out a lawful order, whether written or verbally given. This included contravening the Police Regulations relating to restrictions on the private lives of members, or where an individual was required to notify the chief officer of police that they or a relation had a business interest within the meaning of the Regulations.

A *neglect of duty* involved an offence committed where a member, without good reason, neglected to carry out promptly anything which it was their duty to attend to. The offence could also be committed if an officer failed to work their beat in accordance with orders or left their place of duty. This also applied if, having legitimately left their place of duty, they failed to return without delay. An officer could also be guilty of this offence if they were absent without leave or were late for any duty. Finally, they were similarly guilty if they failed to properly account for or failed to return any money or property received by them in the course of their duty.

An offence of *falsehood or prevarication* occurred if a member of a police force, knowingly or through neglect, made any false, misleading or inaccurate statements or entries in any record required for police purposes. They could similarly be guilty if they, without authority or through lack of care, damaged any such record. An offence was also made out if an officer, without sufficient reason, altered, erased or added to any entry. Finally, an officer offended if they, knowingly or through neglect, made any false, misleading or inaccurate statement in connection with their appointment to the police force.

*Improper disclosure of information* involved cases where an officer without authority released any information which they possessed as a member of a police force. An offence also occurred if an officer without authority contacted the police authority or the council of any county within the police area about matters concerning the force.

*Corrupt or improper practice* took place if an officer, in their capacity as a member of the force and without consent, asked for or accepted any gratuity, present or subscription. An offence could also occur if they placed themselves under an obligation to any person which might affect them properly carrying out their police duties. They were also guilty of an offence if they improperly used their position in the force for personal advantage. The final part of this section involved an offence if an individual gave a character reference so that a person gained employment or was granted any licence.

An *abuse of authority* occurred when an officer, without good reason, made an arrest or used unnecessary force towards anyone with whom they came into contact while on duty or if they were uncivil to any member of the public.

A *neglect of health* referred to situations where an officer neglected to obey a medical officer or, while absent from duty on account of sickness, committed any act which would delay their return to duty.

*Improper dress or untidiness* involved an officer who, while wearing uniform either on or off duty in a public place, was improperly dressed or untidy in their appearance.

*Damage to police property* took place when an officer, either wilfully or through lack of care, caused any damage to police property or failed to report any such damage as soon as possible.

An offence of *drunkenness* was, fairly obviously, alleged to have occurred when an officer was unfit through drink, for duties which they were to perform or could reasonably foresee having to perform.

The offence of *drinking on duty or soliciting drink* is self-explanatory.

*Entering licensed premises* was an offence if an officer, either on duty or off duty but wearing uniform, entered any premises licensed to sell alcohol, or a betting and gaming establishment regulated as a place of entertainment.

An offence of *criminal conduct* was automatic if a court found a member of a police force guilty of a criminal offence.

Finally, *being an accessory to a disciplinary offence* was an offence if an officer was knowingly an accessory to any offence against the discipline code.

In terms of punishments, the officer conducting the hearing was required at its conclusion to either dismiss the charge or find it proven. This decision had to be recorded and notified in writing to the accused officer as soon as possible. Punishments included dismissal from the force; a requirement to resign as an alternative to dismissal; a reduction in rank; a reduction in the rates of pay for a specified period; a fine; a reprimand or a caution.

The language used in this code shows it as somewhat dated and only relevant to a previous era. However, it pretty much existed unaltered until the Police (Performance/Conduct) Regulations of 1999, which in turn have been updated on several occasions, with the most recent version dated 2020.

These more modern standards are directly linked to the Police Code of Ethics which is detailed below. They are very much related to achieving certain standards of behaviour and performance, rather than the repressive feel of the earlier code.

One of the main differences relates to the burden of proof. In the former Discipline Code, any finding of guilt needed to be beyond all reasonable doubt, in other words, identical to the burden of proof required in a criminal court. With the Police (Conduct) Regulations, it is the civil law level of proof, ie on the balance of probabilities. Hearings also differ. In the former Discipline Code, hearings were presided over by either the Chief Constable or the Deputy Chief Constable. The main differences were that, in a Chief's hearing, all punishments were available, whereas in a Deputy's hearings, punishments were restricted to a fine, reprimand or caution. Additionally, in a hearing led by a Chief Constable, legal representation was available to the accused officer. In relation to the later Police (Conduct) Regulations, the hearing is conducted through a tribunal.

First of all, let's look at the Police Code of Ethics, which officers sign up to, from which the Police (Conduct) Regulations and the Police (Performance) Regulations flow.

Police officers should always act with honesty and integrity and ensure they do not compromise or abuse their position. Officers must act with self-control and tolerance and treat members of the public and their colleagues with respect and courtesy. They should use their powers and authority proportionately and lawfully and respect the rights of individuals.

In relation to equality and diversity, officers must act with fairness and impartiality and ensure that they don't discriminate unlawfully or unfairly. They should only use force as part of their role and responsibilities and only to the extent that it is necessary, proportionate and reasonable in all circumstances.

Officers accept they will only give and carry out lawful orders, and in so doing, abide by Police Regulations and always act reasonably. Police officers should always aim to carry out their responsibilities diligently and professionally. They need to respect and understand confidentiality and must treat information with respect, and access or disclose it only in the proper course of their duties.

Police officers are expected to keep themselves fit in order to carry out their responsibilities. Officers must behave in a manner, whether on or off duty, which does not bring discredit on the police service or undermine public confidence in policing.

Officers should report, challenge or take appropriate action as regards the conduct of colleagues which has fallen below the standards of professional behaviour.

It can immediately be seen that this comprises a more modern and simplified version of the previous Police Discipline Code, with a change of emphasis from the negative to the positive – what officers should do, rather than what they shouldn't.

Breaches of the Code of Ethics will not always involve misconduct or require disciplinary proceedings. Breaches will range from relatively minor shortcomings in conduct, performance or attendance, through to gross misconduct and corruption. Different procedures exist according to the type of unprofessional behaviour alleged.

Relatively minor Code breaches may be simply and effectively dealt with through peer or team challenge. Others may require local management action, for example, by a line manager. More significant failures could require formal action by the individual's force or organisation such as, in the case of police officers as opposed to civilian staff, the application of the Police (Conduct) Regulations or the Police (Performance) Regulations.

All officers, staff and, particularly, supervisors and managers have a duty to act where a concern is raised about any behaviour, performance or conduct which may amount to a breach. This is important because this places a certain onus upon officers to act against peers when breaches of the Code of Ethics are apparent.

An example is behaviour that does not uphold policing principles or which falls short of the expected standards set out in this Code. Such matters should be dealt with according to the severity and impact of any suspected breach and at the most appropriate level, as well as in a timely and proportionate manner, to maintain confidence in the process.

Managers and supervisors are expected to exercise professional judgement and consider proportionality in deciding how to deal effectively with alleged unprofessional behaviour. Procedures must be non-discriminatory and handled sensitively and confidentially. Fairness and consistency are therefore important elements. There is no single formula for determining how to deal with a concern about the behaviour or performance of an officer or someone working closely with the police. Each case must be looked at individually and consideration always given to the relevant regulations. Where evidenced or alleged breaches are so serious that the threshold for formal assessment is crossed, such cases should be referred for such action to be taken.

A failure by a police officer to have regard to the standards of professional behaviour in the Code of Ethics may be admissible in evidence in any disciplinary proceedings or in any appeal arising from such proceedings. Similarly, failures by civilian staff members will be dealt with under relevant disciplinary proceedings in their contract of employment.

On an ascending scale of seriousness, actions include self-regulation, local management action and formal assessment and investigation.

Self-regulation is the most important management tool. It relates to the behaviour of officers and that of their immediate peers and teams, through self-awareness and self-challenge; peer awareness and challenge; and team awareness and challenge.

Local management action includes gathering relevant evidence on concerns, discussing any shortcomings with the individual as soon as possible, keeping a note of interactions with the person, and putting the matter on record. The next step is a verbal warning and advice. If there is no improvement, the next stage involves management action, before referral to unsatisfactory performance procedures. Another solution could involve management action as part of a local resolution of a public complaint. Finally, in terms of local management action, this could entail issuing an improvement notice and action plan, redeployment or a temporary change of duty.

A formal assessment and investigation can include management advice, a written warning, a final written warning and dismissal with or without notice. The most serious allegations amounting to gross misconduct can result in suspension from duty or restriction of duty and may involve a criminal investigation and possibly proceedings.

In deciding whether behaviour reflects the Code of Ethics, management must look at the circumstances of the behaviour, given the duties and responsibility of the person; the difference in restrictions on private life between police officers and police staff/other employees/volunteers; the explanation given by the person; the effects of the behaviour on internal or external relationships, the reputation of the police service, their ability to fulfill their duties, and the effects on the organisation's confidence in the individual, and the public's trust in the police.

A severity assessment must be undertaken before deciding whether an officer should face formal misconduct proceedings. The officer's line manager must first be consulted, then the assessor must decide whether the allegation, if proved, would amount to misconduct, gross misconduct or neither. The investigator must also decide whether, if the matter were referred to misconduct proceedings, these would be likely to be a misconduct meeting or a misconduct hearing. At any time before the start of misconduct proceedings, the severity assessment can be reviewed if it seems appropriate to do so.

If it is assessed that the conduct would amount to neither misconduct or gross misconduct, the investigator must next decide whether the conduct would amount to practice requiring improvement; whether it should be dealt with under the Performance Regulations; or whether no further action is needed. Where no further action is decided, or the matter is referred to be dealt with under the reflective practice review process or the Performance Regulations, officer must be told in writing as soon as practicable.

Once it receives the investigator's report, the appropriate authority must determine whether there is a case to answer. If they find the conduct amounts to neither misconduct nor gross misconduct, they can direct the matter is dealt with under the reflective practice review process. If there is a case to answer, the next decision is whether to bring misconduct proceedings against the officer, and if so, what form the proceedings should take.

As regards outcomes, the disciplinary action available at a misconduct meeting is either a written warning or a final written warning. If the person conducting the misconduct proceedings decides the officer's conduct amounts to gross misconduct, options include a final written warning; reduction in rank; or dismissal without notice. However, if the officer had a written warning or a final written warning in force on the date of the severity assessment, then neither a written warning nor a final written warning can be given.

Where a written warning or final written warning is given, that warning remains in force for eighteen months, in the case of a written warning, or a period of two years, in the case of a final written warning.

Moving onto the Police (Performance) Regulations 2020, there are three stages to go through before the situation is deemed serious enough to warrant formal proceedings. These stages involve meetings between the relevant officer, supervisors and senior managers.

Following the third stage meeting, the tribunal panel must make a finding as to whether the officer's performance has been satisfactory. They must also decide whether the performance during any valid period of the final written improvement notice has been satisfactory or whether it constitutes gross incompetence, unsatisfactory performance or neither.

The panel's written decision must state the finding and their reasons, as well as any outcome which they order. The decision is based on a simple majority but the written findings must not indicate whether it was taken unanimously or by a majority.

As soon as reasonably practicable and certainly before the end of three working days, the panel chair must give a written copy of the decision to the officer concerned, and to the line manager. Where the panel has found unsatisfactory performance or attendance, or gross incompetence, the copy of the decision must be accompanied by a written notice setting out how the officer may appeal under the Police Appeals Tribunals Rules 2020.

If the panel finds that the performance of the officer has been unsatisfactory, they may order the officer's dismissal with notice, the notice period to be decided by the panel, subject to a minimum period of twenty-eight days; the dismissal of the officer concerned with immediate effect; a reduction in rank with immediate effect; an extension of the period of the existing final written improvement notice; the issue of a final written improvement notice; the redeployment of the officer to other duties (which may involve a reduction of rank) within the police force concerned.

The panel may not order a reduction in rank with immediate effect where the officer is a special constable, or the third stage meeting relates to the attendance of the officer.

In considering whether to order any of these outcomes, the panel must have regard to the service record of the officer and may receive evidence from any witness which would, in their opinion, assist their consideration. Also, they must give the officer, the officer's police friend or the officer's relevant lawyer, and the appropriate authority, an opportunity to make oral or written representations before they make a decision.

If the panel finds unsatisfactory performance, they must order the issue of a written improvement notice. Such a notice, either final or not, must state how the officer's performance is considered unsatisfactory or grossly incompetent. They must also state the improvement that is required. They also need to make clear that, if sufficient improvement is not made and maintained within a period the panel specifies (up to twelve months), the officer may be required to attend a second stage meeting (in the case of a written improvement notice) or another third stage meeting (in the case of a final written improvement notice) and state the date with which this period ends. This documentation must be signed and dated by the panel chair. The same conditions apply where the panel orders an extension of the period of the final written improvement notice.

The purpose of detailing the various regulations has been to highlight to the reader what is in place to deal with corruption and misconduct committed by police officers. Additionally, of course, police officers could, in the most serious cases, be prosecuted through the criminal courts. In such cases, there are provisions to either deal with misconduct hearings without prejudicing those criminal proceedings or putting them on hold pending the conclusion of criminal cases.

So what constitutes corruption and misconduct within the police and why does it happen? It is interesting that, when talking to non-police people, the response inevitably mentions the taking of backhanders. Whilst this still happens, the manifestations of corruption are many and varied. In the past, there were good examples of senior police officers 'being in the pocket' or 'on the payroll' of certain top-level criminals and being paid considerable sums of money to either turn a blind eye to criminal conduct, pass police information or worse still, actively participate in the commission of criminal offences.

The issue of 'noble cause' corruption will be dealt with fully later. However, it has been shown that disillusionment with the organisation and being overlooked for specific roles or promotion have served to turn the heads of some serving officers. In the early 2000s in Sussex, a number of chief inspectors, involved in various forms of corrupt behaviour, were identified and sacked. The consistent theme seemed to have been that they were all overlooked for promotion to superintendent. The step up from chief inspector is a significant one, both financially and in terms of levels of responsibility. Having been knocked back several times myself, the effect on me, whilst hugely disappointing, did not eat away at me, but I know that the effects on some people can lead them to become obsessed with such failures. Not only can this make them disillusioned but occasionally, they develop into 'organisational terrorists', undermining the organisation at every opportunity. Arguably it's only a small step from this state of mind to becoming susceptible to corruption.

When one considers susceptibility to corruption from outside elements, it is not necessarily those at the highest levels that are nowadays targeted by criminal gangs. Indeed, trends suggest it is those at the lower levels, often amongst the lowest paid and ironically with direct access to criminal intelligence systems, who are at the greatest risk of being approached by criminals. There have even been cases of criminal gang members forming relationships with junior female staff to access intelligence relating to their activities.

The vetting processes within the police are amongst the most stringent, dependent upon the various roles. During my service, I was DV (Developed Vetted), recognised as the top level, which means the holder can view documents graded *Top Secret*. However, it does need to be recognised that, whilst such vetting levels are held for years and are subject to annual reviews, they really are only as good as the day on which they are completed. To use a similar analogy, it is a little like vetting checks linked to child protection. Just because an individual, with no criminal convictions or with no intelligence to show they are a risk, is deemed a low risk today, that doesn't mean they might not be a risk in the future, indeed even the next day! At the absolute best, vetting processes will only ever identify an individual's susceptibility to illegal approaches. It can never be foolproof, but then, what system can?

Along with vetting processes, other developments have been brought in to deal with alleged corruption or misconduct. Some have been incorporated into legislation. One good example was the Police and Criminal Evidence Act (PACE) 1984. This is probably the most far-reaching piece of legislation to impact on policing practices. The reason for its inception related principally to matters involving police 'stop and search' and also to the interviewing of suspects. Considerable criticism had developed over the years regarding the police use of 'stop and search', in particular the stopping and searching of black youths in London and other major cities. Indeed, the *Scarman Report* of 1981 came about because of the Brixton riots which in turn were linked to the Metropolitan Police operation known as Operation Swamp. During that operation, the police relied on powers known as the 'Sus Laws' which were operated under the somewhat archaic legislation contained within the Vagrancy Act of 1824.

The other major aspect of PACE was the interrogation of suspects. There had been a number of miscarriages of justice linked to what was known as 'verbals' or 'verballing'. This involved police officers inventing either admissions or other damning remarks supposedly made by suspects in order to incriminate them. Before PACE, the existing Judges Rules, set in 1912, made no provision for interviews to be formally recorded verbatim. Evidence contained within police interviews was recorded in a police officer's pocket notebook, 'as soon as practicable after the interview took place'. This was clearly open to potential abuse at worst or at best was only ever a summary recorded from the memory of individual officers. PACE determined that all interviews would be recorded in future.

One of the most notorious cases highlighting this issue involved the murder of Maxwell Confait, briefly mentioned previously. Confait was a male prostitute who was strangled and his body discovered in a burnt out flat in Catford, South London, in 1972.

Three innocent boys were jailed for his murder after making confessions that medical evidence subsequently demonstrated could not have been true.

The three boys had fallen under suspicion after they were picked up by the police on suspicion of lighting a series of fires. Obviously vulnerable due to their mental capacity, with the youngest being just fourteen years old and the eldest eighteen, they were held without a lawyer and without contact with parents. By 2 in the morning and after many hours of oppressive interrogation, they signed their statements, effectively sealing their fates.

The police surgeon and the pathologist initially put the time of Confait's death as somewhere between 8pm and 10pm when the boys had alibis. At trial, they appeared to change their minds, saying that the murder could have happened as late as 1am, a time for which none of the boys had alibis. However, later evidence contradicted this adjusted time, and showed that Confait had been dead for over forty-eight hours and rigor mortis was wearing off. Two eminent forensic pathologists, Professors Alan Usher and Keith Mant, confirmed this conclusion, stressing that the discoloration of the organs of the body at the post-mortem indicated seventy-two hours had passed since death. In 1975, after considerable effort by the boys' families and lawyers, the then Home Secretary Roy Jenkins sent the case back to the Court of Appeal which, in turn, cleared the three.

My final point in this chapter involves an element of corruption which may not be immediately apparent, albeit arguably it exists in many organisations, not just the police. This is the problem of nepotism or favouritism within the senior management structure. Why is this an issue, you may well be asking yourself? My argument is simply this. If such a thing exists at the very top of an organisation, the effects are passed right the way down and breed an extremely unhealthy and oppressive body, especially for those who sit outside the chosen few. It is insidious. During the 1990s, while Paul Whitehouse was Chief Constable of Sussex Police, he ensured that a certain breed of officer was successful in terms of promotion to the highest levels of the force. Indeed, a promotion selection process involving what were known as Assessment Centres was brought in and it was clear that certain individuals were coached to pass through the innumerable hoops placed between them and their next promotion.

What it also meant was the force developed a whole industry in relation to promotion and selection processes, costing many thousands of pounds. What was the issue? Well, it was noticeably clear that it did not achieve what it said it would, ie a better breed of senior officer. Indeed, certainly in its early stages, the process did not include any elements which showed an officer's operational competence. Much more sinister was the fact that there was a group of senior managers who identified individuals who 'fitted their mold' and actively supported them to give them an unfair advantage. Is this a case of sour grapes on my part? Too right it is! However, that does not detract from the dangers of the situation. It was clear that if your face did not fit, even if you could show high levels of operational capability and leadership, you were consistently overlooked. On one occasion, I could show that the line of successful candidates was arbitrarily drawn above my name, thus ensuring I did not progress. I appealed the decision but it did me no good whatsoever and only served to reinforce the view that I was a troublemaker.

I take solace in the fact that, after Paul Whitehouse left the force, I managed to achieve promotion to a very senior level during a different regime, as indeed did others. It could, of course, be argued that this is what happens in life and that different leaders see things differently. However, what happened to Sussex Police under the leadership of Paul Whitehouse shows the folly of 'tinkering' with selection processes. Following the intervention of the then Home Secretary, David Blunkett, Whitehouse was effectively forced to retire, after years of poor performance by the force, which included the fatal shooting of what transpired to be an unarmed man. Additionally, there were several failed high profile murder investigations where criticism had been levelled at the force by outside forces conducting inspections and reviews. To further support my argument, on the back of the shooting just referred to, a review of the performance of the Chief Officer team in Sussex was undertaken independently by Sir John Hoddinott, then Chief Constable of Hampshire Police. His report concluded that the leadership within Sussex Police was poor and not only did Paul Whitehouse have to take early retirement, his deputy, Mark Jordan, was also forced to resign! The removal of both a Chief Constable and Deputy is pretty much unprecedented. The case involving the death of James Ashley, as a result of an armed operation carried out by Sussex Police, will be mentioned again later.

# CHAPTER 2

## Policing the Police

In 1997, with over nineteen years of police service under my belt, I entered Sussex Police's Discipline and Complaints Department. Nowadays, it is known as the Professional Standards Department (PSD). It coincided with a time where efforts were being made to use seasoned detectives in the unit to give it credibility.

It was an interesting and somewhat different time in my police career. For a period of years as Chairman of the Police Federation's local Inspectors Branch Board, I had operated as a 'Federation Friend', which meant I had represented officers in misconduct investigations who potentially faced a full disciplinary hearing. At that time, a hearing consisted of a tribunal chaired by either the force's Chief Constable or the Deputy Chief Constable. The major difference between the two was that the Chief Constable had the power to dismiss officers whilst the Deputy couldn't. At a Deputy's hearing, as a 'Friend', I represented officers as an advocate in much the same way as a solicitor represents an individual in court. With a Chief's hearing, the Federation paid for legal representation in appropriate cases and therefore the 'Friend' operated in much the same way as a solicitor's clerk or junior counsel to a senior barrister (QC). Therefore, my entry into the Discipline and Complaints Department was a little like moving from poacher to gamekeeper! Indeed, this was even more the case because, as a senior detective, I was very much used to employing tactics and investigative techniques to arrest criminals. I would now be using the same skills and knowledge to potentially end the careers of colleagues. However, the job was much more than this and involved showing dispassion and independence to ensure that a balanced investigation took place.

The work of today's PSDs has always been supervised by an independent body. The powers of these bodies have increased over time. Originally, and very much historically, the former Watch Committees, that existed before Police Authorities, oversaw the disciplinary process at local level. Following this, the Police Complaints Board (PCB) was brought in and very much like its successor, the Police Complaints Authority (PCA), had more of an oversight responsibility than hands-on investigation. Indeed, neither body employed investigators and this role was undertaken by police forces themselves through their Discipline and Complaints Departments. On occasions, in serious matters, an independent police force was appointed to conduct the investigation and these were directly supervised by the PCA and were indeed referred to as 'supervised investigations'. We had to await the development of the IPCC or Independent Police Complaints Commission and its current replacement, the IPOC, before we saw the advent of an investigative arm.

## The Police Complaints Board and the Police Complaints Authority

The Police Complaints Board, (PCB) operationally independent of the police, oversaw the system for handling complaints against police forces and officers in England and Wales from June 1977 until it was replaced by the Police Complaints Authority in April 1985. Its creation followed a series of scandals involving the Metropolitan Police in the mid-1970s, and criticism of a perceived lack of independence in the existing process.

Until the creation of the PCB in 1977, complaints against officers were handled directly by the forces concerned, although the Home Secretary could refer a serious complaint to another police force for investigation. In cases involving potential criminal allegations, the investigating force would forward a report to the Director of Public Prosecutions (DPP), who could decide whether or not to prosecute the suspected police officers.

The PCB could scrutinise a report from an investigating force and satisfy itself that justice had been done and instruct the Chief Constable of the force, against whom the complaint had been made, to take disciplinary proceedings against offending police officers, should the evidence justify this. The PCB did not cover Northern Ireland, which was the responsibility of a separate body, the Police Complaints Board for Northern Ireland, also set up under the Police Act 1976. Nor did it cover Scotland, which retained the mechanism set up by the Police (Scotland) Act 1967.

The 1981 Brixton riots and the *Scarman Report* on them which investigated, amongst other things, allegations of racism against the police, led to pressure to reform the PCB. The result was that the board was replaced by the Police Complaints Authority (PCA) in the Police and Criminal Evidence Act 1984 (PACE). A significant change was that the PCA was given extra powers, allowing it to supervise police investigations into complaints. The PCA, its successor the Independent Police Complaints Commission (IPCC) and the present Independent Office for Police Conduct (IOPC) were/are all operationally independent of the British police.

## The Independent Police Complaints Commission

The IPCC was a non-departmental public body in England and Wales, responsible for overseeing the system for handling complaints against police forces in England and Wales. Given the task of increasing public confidence in the complaints system and formally founded in 2003, it replaced the PCA. Funded by the Home Office and based in regional offices in Cardiff, London, Sale and Wakefield, the IPCC operated under statutory powers and duties defined in the Police Reform Act of 2002. It was independent of pressure groups, political parties and, in principle, of government.

The IPCC was overseen by a chair, two deputy chairs, seven operational and three non-operational commissioners. The chair was a Crown appointment and commissioners were public appointments. The operational commissioners and the three non-operational commissioners were appointed by the Home Secretary for a five- or three-year period. Commissioners by law could not have served with the police at any time, been the chair or a member of the Serious Organised Crime Agency (SOCA) at any time or been a commissioner or officer of Customs at any time. They were the public, independent face of the IPCC.

From April 2006, the IPCC took on responsibility for similar, serious complaints against HM Revenue and Customs and SOCA in England and Wales. In April 2008, it additionally took on responsibility for serious complaints against UK Border Agency staff.

The IPCC could elect to manage or supervise police investigations into particular complaints or could independently investigate the most serious cases itself. It set standards for police forces to improve the way the public's complaints were handled and also handled appeals by the public about the way their complaint was dealt with by the local force, or its outcomes.

Between April 2004 and March 2009, the IPCC ran 353 independent and 759 managed investigations into the most serious complaints against the police. There were several types of incidents that the police, or other agencies the IPCC oversaw, had to mandatorily refer to the commission. These included deaths in police custody, shootings and fatal traffic incidents, as well as allegations that an officer or member of police staff had committed a serious criminal offence. Forces could also refer matters voluntarily to the IPCC and the commission could 'call in' any matter where there might have been serious public concern.

As well as employing its own independent investigators, often ex-police officers, to investigate the most serious cases, the IPCC had staff performing several other functions. Once a matter was referred to them, the IPCC would make a 'mode of investigation' decision to decide how it should be dealt with. Caseworkers usually recorded the details and assessed the case before recommending a method of investigation, which would then be passed to a Commissioner for sign off. The assessment involved judging the available information and could mean IPCC investigators were sent to the scene. Most complaints were referred back to the PSD of the police force the complaint was about. However, the IPCC's independent investigators investigated the most serious complaints, for example, where someone died following contact with the police.

In April 2017, the IPCC became responsible for oversight of complaints in relation to the Gangmasters and Labour Abuse Authority_and from 2018, in certain circumstances, took responsibility for oversight of complaints in relation to fire and rescue service personnel.

The four modes of investigation were as follows. Firstly, in descending order of seriousness, there were the *independent investigations* carried out by the IPCC's own investigators and overseen by an IPCC Commissioner. In an independent investigation, the IPCC investigators had all the powers and privileges of a police constable in relation to that investigation throughout England and Wales. *Managed investigations* were carried out by police PSDs, under the direction and control of the IPCC. There were also what were referred to as *supervised investigations* carried out by police PSDs, under their own direction and control. The IPCC would set the terms of reference for a supervised investigation and receive the investigation report when it was complete. Complainants had a right of appeal to the IPCC following a supervised investigation. Finally, there were *local investigations* carried out entirely by police PSDs, or by other officers on their behalf. Complainants had a right of appeal to the IPCC following a local investigation.

Should new information emerge after a mode of investigation had been decided, the IPCC could change the classification, both up and down the scale.

On 27 June 2012, the Home Affairs Committee announced an inquiry into the IPCC itself, including, but not limited to, analysis of its independence, its powers and responsibilities, and the effectiveness of its investigations. The Committee began hearing evidence in July 2012. The report, published in January 2013, was scathing, describing it as 'woefully under-equipped and hamstrung in achieving its original objectives. It has neither the powers nor the resources that it needs to get to the truth when the integrity of the police is in doubt.'

## Independent Office for Police Conduct

The Independent Office for Police Conduct (IOPC) is similarly a non-departmental public body in England and Wales which, since 8 January 2018, has been responsible for overseeing the system for handling complaints made against police forces in England and Wales.

The IOPC originated from the Policing and Crime Act in 2017 and, unlike its IPCC predecessor, does not have a commission structure. Instead, it is headed by a Director General, supported by Deputies, Regional Directors and a Director for Wales. The Act also furnished the IOPC with powers the IPCC did not have, such as the power to initiate its own investigations without relying on a force to record and refer; powers to determine appeals and recommend remedies; and a shortened process for deciding whether a case should go to a disciplinary hearing.

Most allegations are still investigated by police forces' own PSDs (with oversight by the IOPC). However, the IOPC, like its predecessor, the IPCC, does conduct independent investigations of serious allegations of misconduct or criminal offences by police officers and other law enforcement officers.

Mandatory referrals are usually made to the IOPC should a person die or in cases involving serious injuries following police contact. Additionally, a force's PSD may also make a voluntary referral, in which a force will ask the IOPC to consider if they wish to investigate independently, supervise a force professional standards investigation, or decline and refer the investigation back to the force to investigate without any IOPC input.

The overriding principle surrounding the creation of each of these entities has been to develop levels of independence from police forces and police officers themselves. However, in trying to achieve this, things have run far from smoothly. The same type of criticisms levelled at the former IPCC are now made against the IOPC. The Police Federation in particular has been scathing, at times, of both the quality of investigations and especially the huge amounts of time taken to complete these. Some have gone on for years and this is fair to neither accused officers nor indeed complainants and their families.

One of the reasons for this is that, in trying to show complete impartiality and independence from the police, they have lost the confidence of officers, because they appear to tackle investigations from the viewpoint of 'guilty until proven innocent' - in other words, the complete opposite of how things should be. This is the view of many associated with the police, as well as many who work within the legal profession.

Additionally, the abilities of the current crop of IOPC investigators leave a lot to be desired. In past years, the IPCC employed a number of former police officers. Those investigating complaints against, and misconduct involving, police officers surely need a fundamental understanding of policing and what it involves. This enables an investigator to understand why things may have happened as they have, thus perhaps offering an altogether different explanation for a given set of circumstances. In other words, things are not always as they appear.

During my two and a half years working in the Discipline and Complaints Department (D&C), I came across all sorts. There were the arrogantly criminal officers who were patently dishonest, there were the criminally stupid, and then there were those who had simply made a mistake. However, whenever I began an investigation, I always took the standpoint that there may be an alternative explanation for what appeared to be even the most obvious set of circumstances. As a result, in particular where an officer may have been innocent or had made genuine mistakes, just trying to do their best, I found they were much more inclined to fully co-operate. They trusted me, regardless of the circumstances. That trust does not exist with the current set up. As a result, all too often, a very unsuccessful outcome is inevitable where officers are not found to be innocent and on the other hand, a case that should have been proven against them isn't, thus leaving complainants totally dissatisfied. Put another way, it can be argued that you need to 'use a thief to catch one', albeit not literally! This is another version of the so-called 'poacher turned gamekeeper'. However, you definitely need someone who understands how things work, both in terms of systems and processes, as well as what police officers may do in certain circumstances.

Let's look at a case I investigated. It involved the wife of a serving officer who made allegations against him involving physical assault as well as sexual assault amounting to rape. She came to us with what on the face of it was a totally plausible version of events. Indeed, she was supported by a friend, a professional woman in terms of her occupation. To all intents and purposes, it was a sad story where the complainant stated she was undergoing treatment for cancer. Her friend described how the complainant had shown her a handful of her own hair, saying it was falling out due to chemotherapy. At this time, she and her husband were still together.

Right from the outset, I made sure no stone was left unturned and I set out to investigate the matter as I would have done if it did not involve a serving police officer. I spoke with all those who had contact with the wife and they confirmed what she had told me about her illness as well as the assault allegations. Her husband, the serving officer, was interviewed in the presence of a solicitor and all the allegations were put to him. He vehemently denied these, stating that, while he and his wife were going through a difficult time, he was innocent. He was advised to leave the marital home, which he did whilst the investigation was ongoing, and he was suspended from duty because of the seriousness of the allegations.

However, his wife then stated he had returned to the house, forced his way in and assaulted her physically. There was evidence of bruising around her face. He was again interviewed but could provide an airtight alibi. I was now deeply suspicious of the wife's allegations. I tried to ascertain the details of the hospital and the name of the doctor treating her. She gave the name of the hospital but claimed she couldn't remember the doctor's name. When I contacted the hospital, they could find no record of her.

I obtained authority to install a covert camera opposite her home, in the event that her husband should allegedly return. Incredibly, she contacted the police late one night to say her husband had tried to force his way in but had left. She indicated some scratches and marks on her face and neck and said these had been inflicted by her husband. When I retrieved the camera footage, it showed only the complainant coming out of her house at the given time and then returning inside. Once again, I made enquiries as to where her husband was at the time – as before, he was a considerable number of miles away, staying at another address which was confirmed.

Despite the overwhelming evidence which showed the complainant had invented the whole story, she refused to admit the facts. The whole thing was quite incredible, especially when one considers that she had clearly pulled out her own hair and inflicted injuries upon herself to corroborate the assault allegations. Through her friend, I tried to have her visit her own doctor in relation to what clearly amounted to mental health problems. The case showed the importance of retaining an open mind when conducting such investigations. Who would have thought that anyone could invent such an elaborate set of circumstances?

The very first serious case that I became involved in with the D&C was somewhat unusual, to say the least. Together with a colleague, we investigated a police sergeant who was involved in transporting handguns from this country to France, on behalf of others. He had set himself up to do this, running it as a business, following a change in firearms legislation. By doing this, it meant that individuals could go over to France and use their weapons in the normal way in accordance with gun laws in that country. There were two main issues. Firstly, the law did not allow him to transport weapons. Secondly, he was a police officer with an undeclared business interest. Police officers can apply to have a business interest and a decision will be taken as to whether such an interest is compatible with their role as a police officer. Clearly, in this case, there is no way that such permission would ever have been granted.

Interestingly, the individual concerned was a former firearms officer in the Metropolitan Police and had fairly recently transferred to Sussex. Therefore, he was something of an expert in the use and handling of firearms. However, legally, he had no right in law to be transporting them.

We put in place an undercover operation involving two officers who contacted the sergeant via the advertised phone number, saying they had weapons they wished him to take to France. This is what is known as a 'test purchase'. Having obtained the necessary evidence through this means, the target was arrested. During a search of his premises, a quantity of 9mm ammunition was discovered which, from the serial numbers, was traced to the Metropolitan Police, who, surprisingly and worryingly, couldn't provide an audit trail for this ammunition! All firearms and ammunition allocated to officers, for obvious reasons, must be signed out and signed back in, if unused in the case of ammunition.

The sergeant ultimately appeared at a Chief Constable's hearing and was dismissed from the force, though we could never prove the theft of the ammunition due to the Met's poor record keeping. I suspect that some of the reason for this was due to the inevitable embarrassment.

This case highlights an arrogant criminal intent on the part of a police officer where an individual totally disregards their responsibilities to both the law and the strict disciplinary codes which allow the force to operate.

Other cases followed the same pattern. We received information that there was an officer who was selling large amounts of good quality clothing to friends and colleagues. We executed a search warrant at his home and recovered huge quantities of clothes, none of which bore any labels. He had no receipts for these and there were far too many items for one individual to wear. Indeed, there were hundreds consisting of jeans, casual trousers, shirts and jackets.

He was interviewed under caution on suspicion of theft which he denied. Further enquiries revealed that, in all likelihood, the items had come from a local Debenhams store where, it transpired, an associate of the officer worked. We could never prove the theft, but the store management knew they had stock shortfalls. The officer concerned was allowed to resign. This again reveals a level of arrogance which suggests that certain officers believe they can operate this way without their misdemeanors being discovered.

I experienced something similar when I received a tip off from a colleague, suggesting that a named chief inspector had been misusing his force credit card to make private purchases. When this was looked into, it was very clear he had been doing exactly that. Indeed, he had even been entertaining female colleagues by buying meals and booking hotel rooms. The fact that the credit card misuse had gone unnoticed for so long showed how lax the force's accounting systems were. This was rectified very quickly!

He was interviewed and then allowed to resign, a satisfactory outcome for many such cases when they do not involve a member of the public. It saves a considerable amount of time and prevents officers being suspended on full pay at the tax payer's expense, pending a formal hearing. Such decisions are always taken in consultation with the CPS, in the case of potential criminal matters, and/or the PCA, as it was when I was a part of D&C.

Having covered the arrogantly criminal, let's move to the downright stupid. The first case involved a police sergeant who, it transpired, was visiting a prostitute in duty time! The local CID had been conducting observations on a premises occupied by a known prostitute and believed to have been associated with the dealing of Class A drugs. During this operation and on two separate occasions, the sergeant concerned was seen entering the premises and then leaving around an hour later.

I interviewed the officer in the presence of his Federation Friend, during which he admitted that he had been visiting the prostitute in duty time. After consultation with senior colleagues, he was once again allowed to resign immediately.

My final example is quite funny in its own way. I received a phone call suggesting that an officer, who had been off sick for several months, was operating a fast-food van on a local industrial estate. On this occasion, I went to the location already prepared with the necessary misconduct paperwork. I had a photograph of the officer to correctly identify him and I sat in my car to watch the vehicle from which he was allegedly operating. Sure enough, there he was, serving the public with hot dogs and burgers! I decided to buy one myself. After all, what better evidence could I obtain? Having made my purchase, I took him to one side and served the necessary forms upon him, together with a pre-

prepared letter of resignation which he duly signed. In his case, he was not only working whilst on sick leave but also had an undeclared business interest. For the record, the burger was particularly good!

Inevitably, the media seem to have become obsessed with cases involving what can loosely be referred to as police brutality or, to use the correct terminology, excessive use of force. Much of D&C's caseload involved such allegations and in most of these cases, there was no case to answer. Even where police officers were seen on CCTV striking individuals prior to arrest, this does not necessarily amount to excessive force. This is because there is a need to understand the context.

My entry into D&C coincided with the introduction of the long-handled, and then subsequently extendable, police baton. Before then, the police had traditional wooden truncheons. With the introduction of the newer form of baton came a major difference in training for its use. Rather than using it defensively, it was used offensively, should the correct circumstances prevail. If violence was being offered by suspects, it now became perfectly legitimate to use particular 'strikes' to the offender's body to gain control of them. When viewed on CCTV, of course this inevitably did not look good and went against most people's perception of the police. Indeed, at this time, a lot of police equipment changed completely and became somewhat militaristic in appearance.

PCA members had real difficulty in understanding how something that appears to be a violent act carried out by a police officer was, in fact, legitimate use of force on most occasions. Indeed, because all of this was so new, it became normal, when submitting a file to the PCA for their consideration, to include a statement from a staff safety trainer, detailing how they viewed what was seen in the video.

However, when it comes to the use of force and what is and is not justifiable, there are examples of the unbelievably bad. One of the worst occurred in August 1983 and was widely covered in the media and even the Houses of Parliament.

On Saturday night, 6 August 1983, an elite Met Police team, November 33, from the District Support Unit (DSU) was patrolling the streets of North London. The DSUs were the second generation of the Met's specialist public order units and clearly their role was 'never that they should roam around the streets together in a van looking for trouble'. They had earlier visited a fair at Highbury Fields and were apparently taunted by some boys. It was later claimed the eight officers had 'resolved corporately to extract some revenge, and to alleviate the boredom of what had turned out that day to be a double shift'. The boys, having left the fair and aware of the police van following them, ran along Holloway Road and into Georges Road, where the van caught up with them. Officers immediately lined the boys up against some railings where the five schoolboys, aged from thirteen to sixteen, found themselves 'the victims of a sudden, quick and ferocious attack from the fists, feet and truncheons of officers...' Serious injuries were sustained by the boys, ranging from fractures to deep cuts, shocking bruises and abrasions. One of the boys said these police officers simply 'steamed into us'.

The eight officers sped off immediately after the attack. Not even one 'reported the incident to their superior officers'. One of the officers involved in the attack, PC Gavin, later told investigators, 'When we got back in the van, everyone treated it as a vast joke. There was talk of doing it again. It was treated as fun.'

The Met's Complaints Investigation Bureau (CIB2) sought to find the officers responsible but for two and half years, the eight offending officers were not identified. November 33 was one of three DSU teams in the area that night. Despite two teams not being involved in the horrific beatings, all three units conspired to build a wall of silence so investigators could never hope to find those responsible.

More than three years after the assault, in February 1986, three officers finally came forward. Under the prospect of immunity, they identified the correct police unit, November 33, whose eight officers were PCs Kevin Luxford, Derek Jamieson, Phillip Boak, Edward Main, Michael Gavin, Nicholas Wise, Michael Parr and Sergeant Colin Edwards. Of these eight, five were eventually sentenced for their heinous crimes.

At this point, the *Police Review* magazine persuaded Scotland Yard to end its silence over the affair and announce that they had found the officers responsible for the atrocity. The editor of *Police Review*, Brian Hilliard, referred to those involved as being 'a conspiracy of bastards'.

The following extract appeared in a news report dated 8 February 1986:

> A group of policemen who beat up five teenage boys in Holloway, North London two and a half years ago caused enormous harm to the reputation of the Metropolitan Police, according to this week's Police Review. A leading article in the magazine describes the policemen as "bastards" and asks why no officer was prepared to denounce them. The consequences of this silence are immeasurable. The assaulted youths, their families, their friends, can never again trust a police officer.

The trial of November 33's officers took place at the Old Bailey in July 1987. On 16 July, the judge directed the terms of punishment for the attack on the five Holloway boys. Mr Justice Kenneth Jones said the officers of the November 33 unit had been engaged in a 'disgraceful episode' and behaved 'like vicious hooligans and lied like common criminals'. PCs Edward Main, Michael Gavin and Nicholas Wise received four years each for assault and conspiring to pervert the course of justice. Sergeant Colin Edwards received three years for perverting the course of justice, gross misconduct, failing to protect the victims and not reporting the incident. PC Michael Parr was jailed for eighteen months for perverting the course of justice.

In passing verdict, Mr Justice Jones commented further: 'This was a brutal, bullying and unprovoked attack upon innocent schoolboys. They had given you no particular trouble. Yet you turned upon them and beat them brutally. By these assaults, you have betrayed your own manhood and you have been false to the high traditions of the Metropolitan Police.' The judge added that 'you were prepared to allow suspicion to fall upon your brother officers in the Metropolitan Police to save your own skins' and finally, 'you all conspired to lie and lie again, and you did nothing to repair the damage you knew you had done.'

PCs Kevin Luxford and Phillip Boak, two of the three officers who had revealed the identities of the perpetrators, both admitted lying and conspiring to conceal the truth, but were not disciplined, instead being advised 'their usefulness as coppers is at an end and the sooner they clear off the better'. The third, PC Derek Jamieson, had already heeded this popular opinion and resigned from the police. Compensation was paid out of court to at least three of the boys, consisting of a somewhat paltry £1,000.

It transpired PC Edward Main had been involved in an attack upon a victim prior to the Holloway Boys case and had been allowed to continue as a serving officer, despite the Met Police having to pay out damages to the unknown victim for the assault.

Deputy Assistant Commissioner Peter Winship, apologising on behalf of the Met, said these officers 'disgraced the proud reputation' of police and 'angered the many thousands of officers who each day perform loyal service to the people of London'. He added that the attack had been a serious departure from the high standards expected and the fact 'that it was accompanied by a prolonged conspiracy to conceal the truth is a matter of even deeper concern'.

One of the findings from the Old Bailey trial was that the Met's DSU teams were comprised of inexperienced officers who were simply in a 'habit of driving around together and, effectively, hunting in a pack'. This led to calls for the DSUs to be disbanded. However, they were replaced with the Territorial Support Group (TSG), which many considered equally troublesome. The DSU itself had replaced the earlier Special Patrol Group (or SPG), itself historically involved in the death of Blair Peach at Southall in 1979. These changes were implemented by the Met in the hope the new units would be free of any paramilitary image or reputation. One other result from the case was that all police vehicles would, from then on, be identified by numbers on their roofs and sides so that they could easily be picked out.

The horrific assault even came up in Parliamentary debates. Here's one example from Hansard, 24 July 1987:

> Mr Chris Smith asked the Secretary of State for the Home Department if he will indicate the numbers of police officers, by rank and department, who were assigned to investigate the assault in August 1983 of five youngsters in Georges Road Holloway, at each stage of the three investigations into the incident; and what were the dates on which their report was submitted and to whom.
>
> Mr Douglas Hogg: The first investigation was conducted by a detective chief inspector who reported on 16 March 1984. The second was conducted by a detective chief inspector who reported on 24 August 1984. The third was conducted by a detective chief superintendent who reported on 12 February and 23 April 1985. Each of these officers was attached to the Metropolitan Police Complaints Investigation Bureau and was assisted by a detective sergeant throughout his investigation and by other officers from time to time as the need arose. Their reports were submitted to the commander of the Complaints Investigation Bureau. In February 1986, the Commissioner of Police of the Metropolis instituted a further investigation

of the case. This was led by a Deputy Assistant Commissioner who was assisted by a team of officers and civilian staff. The size of this team varied in accordance with particular requirements, but at one time included over twenty individuals.

Interestingly, I have recently read a fictional account, written by a former Metropolitan Police officer named Mike Thomas entitled *Ugly Bus*. The book portrayed a group of officers working together in a police van who regularly conducted themselves as the officers involved in the Holloway Road incident did.

The work of Professional Standards Departments, as they are now known, is critical in ensuring that officers maintain the standards expected of serving police officers. A robust system for investigating those guilty of misconduct or corruption is required to ensure public confidence is maintained. Once the trust between police and public is lost, then sadly, the rule of law is called into question and, potentially at least, co-operation between police and policed will inevitably be eroded. The time I spent in the former Discipline and Complaints Department opened my eyes to the extent where, potentially at least, the confidence I had possessed since the early days of my service - that most police officers did a good job - was, to some extent, damaged. By the time I moved on, it was particularly important I should do so. I had reached a point where, on occasions, I doubted the authenticity of complaints against officers made by the public and similarly, I often felt that officers were being less than truthful. Of course, neither statement was actually completely true but there is a definite shelf life for those involved in investigating police officers. My concern is that those employed by the IOPC to investigate such matters are unable to move out of that environment because they are directly employed for that role within the IOPC, whereas police officers in PSDs can move on to take up other roles.

# CHAPTER 3

## Misconduct or Poor Performance and the Links

The police themselves occasionally become confused between misconduct and poor performance, and the differences between them. While certain behaviour might appear to show signs of misconduct, these clues are not always clear and it is up to supervisors and managers to find out the true cause of the problem. Failure to distinguish between misconduct and poor performance can lead to taking the wrong approach.

Poor performance often appears as an inability to fulfill the standards and expectations of the role; a failure to ensure work is completed within a required time frame; and repeated errors in work. Some cases of poor performance are unintentional. On occasions, a police officer or staff member will be unaware they are under-performing and won't change unless they are told otherwise.

The most common reasons for under-performance include misunderstanding the standards and expectations for the job; not enough training or support; personal reasons or sickness; work-related stress; workplace bullying; and low morale or job satisfaction.

Misconduct, on the other hand, is behaviour in the workplace which is unacceptable and breaches the Police Code of Ethics, whether a police officer or member of staff, and also contravenes the policies and procedures of a force.

Common examples of misconduct include repeated lateness; poor personal presentation; behaving inappropriately towards other officers/staff; misuse of police computers and personal social media accounts; making threatening and abusive statements or gestures; drug and alcohol abuse in the workplace; theft and corruption.

# GOOD COP BAD COP

It can be hard to tell the difference between misconduct and poor performance at first. However, the differences are quite simple. The reality is misconduct has more to do with a person's behaviour, while poor performance involves their ability to do their job. An officer who is good at their job can still take part in misconduct, such as becoming involved in corrupt activity.

To establish whether a situation involves misconduct or poor performance, it is important to consider the following questions in relation to the police officer's role. Firstly, is the quality of work acceptable? Are they putting in enough effort to complete the job? Is it a form of negligence, 'I don't care', as opposed to intentional misconduct?

If the answer is 'no' to any of these questions, it could be a performance issue and should be handled as such in accordance with the Code of Ethics and the Police (Performance) Regulations 2020. Regarding misconduct, any police force will rely on the Code of Ethics, as well as local orders and policies, to identify what constitutes unacceptable behaviour.

A good example of these issues arose in what became known as the Hillsborough Disaster. Saturday 15 April 1989 dawned bright and sunny. More than fifty-three thousand Liverpool and Nottingham Forest supporters were looking forward to watching their teams compete in the FA Cup Semi-final at Hillsborough, Sheffield. Semi-final day is one of the major dates in the football calendar but this date would sadly be remembered as the biggest human tragedy in UK football history. It was one of those days where many of us would know exactly what we were doing when the news first broke that ninety-six Liverpool fans had died after they were crushed within Sheffield Wednesday's stadium.

The fans who died had been in two pens of the Leppings Lane terrace. Each pen was separated by fences, including an overhanging barrier designed to prevent pitch invasions, and had a small, locked gate that opened onto the pitch. The report, compiled by the Hillsborough Independent Panel, said that, despite obvious signs of distress, it was a while before the police fully reacted and launched attempts to rescue those who were being crushed. Therefore, the police response was highlighted as an issue.

The report further stated that, 'It is evident... that the safety of the crowd admitted to the terrace was compromised at every level: access to the turnstiles from the public highway; the condition and adequacy of the turnstiles; the management of the crowd by South Yorkshire Police (SYP) and the Sheffield Wednesday FC (SWFC) stewards; alterations to the terrace, particularly the construction of pens; the condition and placement of crush barriers; access to the central pens via a tunnel descending at a 1 in 6 gradient; emergency egress from the pens via small gates in the perimeter fence; and lack of precise monitoring of crowd capacity within the pens. These deficiencies were well known and further overcrowding problems at the turnstiles in 1987 and on the terrace in 1988 were additional indications of the inherent dangers to crowd safety. The risks were known and the crush in 1989 was foreseeable.'

The flaws in responding to the emerging crisis on the day were rooted in institutional tension within and between organisations.

The report stated that, 'This was reflected in a policing and stewarding mindset predominantly concerned with crowd disorder; the failure to realise the consequences of opening exit gates to relieve congestion at the turnstiles; the failure to manage the crowd's entry and allocation between the pens; the failure to anticipate the consequences within the central pens of not sealing the tunnel; the delay in realising that the crisis in the central pens was a consequence of overcrowding rather than crowd disorder. The SYP decision to replace the experienced match commander... just weeks before an FA Cup semi-final, has been previously criticised. None of the documents disclosed to the panel indicated the rationale behind this decision.'

Looking at the history, the report went on to say that, 'Throughout the 1980s there was considerable ambiguity about South Yorkshire Police's and Sheffield Wednesday FC's crowd management responsibilities within the stadium. The management of the crowd was viewed exclusively through a lens of potential crowd disorder, and this ambiguity was not resolved despite problems at previous semi-finals. SWFC and SYP were unprepared for the disaster that unfolded on the terraces on 15 April 1989. Not only was there delay in recognising that there were mass casualties, but the major incident plan was also not correctly activated and only limited parts were then put into effect. As a result, rescue and recovery efforts were affected by lack of leadership, coordination, prioritisation of casualties and equipment.'

Referring to the immediate response, the report stated, 'The emergency response to the Hillsborough disaster has not previously been fully examined, because of the assumption that the outcome for those who died was irretrievably fixed, long before they could have been helped. It is not possible to establish whether a more effective emergency response would have saved the life of any one individual who died. Given the evidence disclosed to the panel of more prolonged survival of some people with partial asphyxiation, however, a swifter, more appropriate, better-focused and properly equipped response had the potential to save more lives.'

The report covered the issue of the 'cut-off' referred to in the original inquest and said, 'During the inquest, the coroner ruled that there should be a cut-off of 3.15pm on the day in relation to medical evidence, arguing that the fate of all those who died after this point had already been determined by earlier events. [The 'cut-off' was a term used by the coroner in the original inquest. He, controversially as it transpired, wanted to ignore any events after this time because he felt that all the victims would have been dead by this time]. The panel's access to all the relevant records has confirmed that the notion of a single, unvarying and rapid pattern of death in all cases is unsustainable. Some of those who died did so after a significant period of unconsciousness during which they might have been able to be resuscitated, or conversely may have succumbed to a new event such as inappropriate positioning. It is not possible to establish with certainty that any one individual would or could have survived under different circumstances. It is clear, however, that some people who were partially asphyxiated survived, while others did not. It is highly likely that what happened to these individuals after 3.15pm was significant in determining that outcome. Based on this disclosed evidence, it cannot be concluded that life or death was inevitably determined by events prior to 3.15pm, or that no new fatal event could have occurred after that time.'

With specific criticism of the South Yorkshire Police, it went on, 'It is evident... that from the outset SYP sought to establish a case emphasising exceptional levels of drunkenness and aggression among Liverpool fans, alleging that many arrived at the stadium late, without tickets and determined to force entry.

Eight years after the disaster, it was revealed publicly for the first time that statements made by SYP officers were initially handwritten as "recollections", then subjected to a process of "review and alteration" involving SYP solicitors and a team of SYP officers. Some 116 of the 164 statements identified for substantive amendment were changed to remove or alter comments unfavourable to SYP.

The panel also looked at the allegations of blame levelled against Liverpool fans in some newspapers, including *The Sun*. The documents disclosed to the panel show that the origin of these serious allegations was a local Sheffield press agency informed by several SYP officers, an SYP Police Federation spokesperson and a local MP. They also demonstrate how the SYP Police Federation, supported informally by the SYP Chief Constable, sought to develop and publicise a version of events that focused on several police officers' allegations of drunkenness, ticketlessness and violence among a large number of Liverpool fans. This extended beyond the media to Parliament. Yet, from the mass of documents, television and CCTV coverage disclosed to the panel, there is no evidence to support these allegations, other than a few isolated examples of aggressive or verbally abusive behaviour clearly reflecting frustration and desperation.'

For the inquest juries, police planning errors, stadium defects and delays in the emergency response all contributed to the disaster. The behaviour of the fans was not to blame. Match commander Chief Superintendent David Duckenfield had a duty of care to fans that day, the jurors decided. They found he was in breach of that duty of care, that this amounted to gross negligence and that the ninety-six victims were unlawfully killed.

The jury also concluded that police errors caused a dangerous situation at the turnstiles and that failures by commanding officers caused a crush on the terraces. It decided that there were mistakes in the police control box over the order to open the Leppings Lane end exit gates. They believed that defects at the stadium contributed to the disaster and that there was an error in its safety certification. The police had delayed declaring a major incident and the emergency response, including the ambulance service, was also delayed.

However, what I wish to do is to focus on the event from a police perspective in an effort to demonstrate how, when things go wrong, there is a real danger of facts and perceptions becoming distorted. I also want to show how the pressures on organisations and individuals when blame is being apportioned can affect the way in which they respond.

In recent times, the media have seemingly become obsessed with establishing blame. Take the Grenfell fire disaster. Before the flames had even been extinguished, TV and the wider media were hell bent on establishing who was at fault. This then

*Chief Superintendent David Duckenfield*

inevitably led to a natural inclination for those potentially in the firing line to batten down the hatches and go on the defensive. This in turn brings in the legal profession who wish to achieve 'justice' for the victims and their families, including the potential of a huge financial pay out. Against this will be lawyers doing their best to defend organisations and individuals who may perhaps be culpable, either civilly or criminally. With changes in legislation which allow for bodies and people working within them to be prosecuted for gross negligence manslaughter, there is a lot at stake, including potential loss of liberty if cases are proven.

This can cause a problem and formed a key element of the investigation into the Hillsborough disaster. In the immediate aftermath, the national media were keen to establish who or what was responsible for causing the tragedy. This is understandable to some extent but it set the tone for the months and years that followed. Rather than being a search for the truth, it developed into a witch hunt with the police, other emergency services,

Sheffield Wednesday Football Club and the local authority, all in the firing line. This included senior members within these bodies, some of whom were involved at the front end operationally.

The one name always recalled when Hillsborough is discussed is that of Chief Superintendent David Duckenfield of the South Yorkshire Police, the designated match commander on the day. He has fairly recently finally been acquitted of gross negligence manslaughter charges relating to the deaths of these ninety-six Hillsborough victims. The fact that ultimately, he was the only individual to face criminal charges, other than Graham Mackrell, the then secretary of Sheffield Wednesday, who was convicted of health and safety offences for which he was fined, tells us why it was highly unlikely he would ever be convicted. Maybe David Duckenfield, through his individual failings on the day, did contribute in a major way to what subsequently happened. But there were many other individuals and organisations partially responsible, both on the day and in the lead up to the event, through their individual failure to take seriously enough their responsibilities to hold a safe event, so it would be completely unfair to hold just one person responsible.

It is clear that, immediately following the disaster, things were said and done which were either wholly inaccurate or exaggerated. Readers will recall how the blame in the early stages was laid at the door of Liverpool fans through their behaviour, when some were accused of being drunk, unreasonable and ticketless, leading to them forcing the gates open and the fans being crushed and killed. This accusation was indeed made by David Duckenfield himself, as well as others. This therefore wrongly focused responsibility in the early stages and directly caused battle lines to be drawn, with the whole thing becoming an effort at damage limitation by the authorities. This led to each of them, through lawyers, fighting one another by apportioning blame in different directions. This in turn did nothing to achieve a search for the truth for the victims' families and as a result, even to this day, more than thirty-one years later, they still don't really know what went so badly wrong.

Two key elements arise out of Hillsborough. Firstly, how close a link is there between operational incompetence/performance and corrupt behaviour from a police perspective? Secondly, how, in the aftermath, legal processes can lead people to believe, real or perceived, that corruption or a cover-up has prevailed.

When David Duckenfield got up that morning and prepared himself for the day ahead, he had no intention of performing poorly as the match commander. Unfortunately, he was ill equipped. Shortly before the semi-final, the previous match commander, Chief Superintendent Brian Mole, had arbitrarily been moved by Chief Constable Peter Wright, following what the Chief Constable saw as some ill-discipline in the division under Brian Mole's command.

This probably lies at the heart of what happened on that dreadful day and also what occurred in the aftermath. By his own admission during his trial, David Duckenfield was operationally ill-equipped to take on the match commander role. The fact that he had taken no action on the lead up to the match, to seek the help of his predecessor or any other support, is sadly another thing to his detriment. However, what it meant was that he was unable to adapt to events as they unfolded in front of him and, due to his lack of experience, was unable to use any sort of contingency. Panic set in and he made either poor decisions or, equally as bad, no decisions at all!

In the follow up, it is clear that in effect, Duckenfield either lied or exaggerated what had taken place in order to shift the blame. Whilst this sounds terrible and obviously is, put yourself in that position. You know there have been many fatalities, and everyone is looking at you to provide answers as to how this happened. Such things then lead to a form of self-perpetuation and often an escalation of minor matters. For example, a few Liverpool fans were probably the worse for having drunk too much. Every Saturday afternoon, there are football fans everywhere who do the same thing. Was it so significant that it was a contributory factor to later events? Of course not. Were there Liverpool fans without tickets? Probably and some may have tried to take advantage of the gates being opened by the police to prevent crushing, to gain illegal entry. However, the numbers involved are unlikely to have impacted on subsequent events. You can probably see where this argument is heading. To quote a phrase, 'When the shit is flying, throw some back'. That is undoubtedly what happened in this case. The story then gets exaggerated more and more, *The Sun* gets hold of it and suddenly the blame for the disaster lies with the Liverpool fans. Excusable? No, definitely not. Understandable? Maybe.

One of the key concerns in the days following the disaster was the claim that officers on duty at the semi-final were encouraged or forced to either write their statements in a particular way, emphasising certain points to shift blame, or statements previously made were altered for similar reasons.

There is also little doubt that the mindsets of the media, police and other organisations still focused on events, such as big football matches, as being about crowd control and dealing with hooliganism, rather than about policing a public safety event. This is why, at that time, there were still pens on the terraces of football grounds. It was only four years previously that we had witnessed the Heysel Stadium disaster in Belgium, ironically involving Liverpool fans, when thirty-nine Juventus fans died, prior to the European Cup final. This had led to the banning of English clubs from European football competitions for five years. This background undoubtedly meant that the first thing considered as causing Hillsborough was hooliganism.

In the aftermath of the disaster, the knives were out. Scapegoats were sought and accountability was a key issue. Whilst it may be all right to accept some criticism, there was undoubtedly a constant theme, with the various agencies either shifting or spreading the blame. Once lawyers get involved, things become very messy. There will inevitably be a wish to play down the culpability of organisations and their staff. Place this alongside the police culture prevailing at the time - to admit nothing when it came to accepting responsibility for something that has gone wrong - and you can see immediately why things went the way they did.

Whether this amounts to corruption or some other form of misconduct is a moot point. If it is a case of lawyers seeking opportunities to exploit, to lessen culpability, as unpalatable as this may seem, it is not illegal and therefore cannot be corrupt practice. Some may argue that it amounts to 'gilding the lily' but the legal profession will argue that this is their job. If the issue, on the other hand, involves police officers getting together and 'getting their stories straight', then this will amount to corruption. Similarly, if senior officers encourage or indeed force subordinates to invent evidence or change what was originally stated, to the extent where it amounts to a falsehood, then clearly this is also corrupt. What all this breeds is suspicion in the media which then passes to the public. In this case, clearly the Liverpool fans and families of the deceased became increasingly suspicious and inevitably believed that a cover-up was taking place. Sadly, this whole thing amounted to an attempt to tell a favourable story rather than a search for the truth.

My purpose in exploring the Hillsborough disaster is to show that not everything is always as it seems. What on the face of it appears to be a straightforward cover-up, and therefore a corrupt response, is not always so. There are many other things at play. In the case of Hillsborough, innumerable issues lay behind what ultimately accounted for the tragic deaths of ninety-six people.

The case involving the death by shooting, carried out by Sussex police officers in January 1998, of the unarmed James Ashley is worthy of mention here. This incident came about during a police investigation into the alleged drug dealing activities of Ashley, a man with a criminal history. Intelligence suggested that Ashley was in possession of a handgun in his flat in St Leonards on Sea, East Sussex. As a result of the perceived strength of this intelligence, an armed police operation to search Ashley and his flat took place in the early hours of the morning. When the armed officers entered the flat in darkness, Ashley was naked in front of the door. His girlfriend was in bed. A shot was fired by an armed officer and Ashley was fatally injured.

I was involved in the immediate aftermath as a member of the Discipline and Complaints Department (now Professional Standards). Together with a colleague, I conducted an initial recorded interview with Ashley's girlfriend at Hastings Police Station. Within a short time, a decision was taken by the then Police Complaints Authority (PCA), to have Kent Police investigate the circumstances of Ashley's death. It was the norm at the time to appoint an independent police force to investigate such matters because, unlike the current IOPC, the PCA did not have their own investigative capability. Right from the outset, it seemed as if Kent Police trusted absolutely no one and nothing related to Sussex Police. This may have had something to do with the fact that, early that morning, Sussex Chief Constable Paul Whitehouse had spoken to the media, suggesting that his officers had acted entirely appropriately, and the implication therefore was that there were unlikely to be any issues found as a result. This, of course, negatively affected the PCA's attitude and as a result no doubt, also that of the officers from Kent Police who were tasked with conducting the investigation. Indeed, James Ashley's family made a formal complaint against Paul Whitehouse which ultimately led to the departure from the force of him and his deputy, Mark Jordan.

The point of raising this here is that, without a shadow of doubt, the initial stance of the Sussex force led Kent Police and probably the PCA to believe that corruption in the form of a cover-up was happening. This was exacerbated when it came to the issue of Kent Police testing the strength of the intelligence, used in an effort to justify the armed police operation. The outcome was that suspicion abounded and even I, on the relative periphery of the matter, felt I was being treated as potentially corrupt. I am not sure that such a stance by the investigating force was entirely productive. Ultimately, several officers faced a criminal trial, including the officer who fired the fatal shot, as well as those involved in the gathering, management and dissemination of the intelligence. All were subsequently acquitted. However, the impact on the force was considerable, and as a result, we suffered for over two years until a new senior command team was appointed.

Personally, at times, I felt under siege, not only because of the various interviews I had with the Kent officers but also because I was interviewed by Sir John Hoddinott who conducted a separate investigation related to the effectiveness of the senior command team of Sussex Police. I, and one or two others, became almost paranoid and we ensured that all relevant notebooks and documentation pertaining to the various investigations were stored in a safe within the D&C's offices. As I have said, corruption is a strange thing. Even when you are completely innocent, you can be made to feel as if you yourself are in the firing line!

To tell the full story and show how close Sussex Police and some of its officers, including the Chief Constable and his deputy, came to being guilty of corruption, this extract from Hansard is particularly useful.

> Hansard House Of Commons, Monday 11 February 2002
>
> Louise Ellman MP (Liverpool, Riverside): The fatal shooting of the sleeping unarmed James Ashley at around 4.20am on 15 January 1998, when five of a group of twenty-five heavily armed police burst into his Hastings flat,

demonstrates the failings of Sussex police, the inadequacy of police accountability and a lack of concern for the bereaved.

A single bullet fired at point blank range by Police Constable Chris Sherwood killed James Ashley, aged thirty-nine, as he stumbled out of bed dazed by the light of the torch shone by the raiding police. No arms or drugs were found on the premises, contrary to the information on which authorisation for the raid rested.

Jimmy Ashley's family are my constituents. I have witnessed their deep grief at their loss but that grief has been followed by anger and incredulity that no one has been brought to account for the needless death. Indeed, in the four years since, little has been revealed in the public sphere, little action has been taken, no one has been brought to account for what happened and it looks as if few lessons have been learned.

The Ashleys first heard of Jimmy's killing through a chance television and teletext viewing. Indeed, at one stage a neighbour who had been listening to the radio approached them. They heard that someone who answered the description of their son had been shot dead by police in an area of Hastings where they knew their son lived. No name was given at that stage but they suspected that something was wrong.

The family made a series of telephone calls to Sussex police, to coroners and to a range of other individuals and organisations. They were given little information and even less help. They were never officially informed that James Ashley had died and they have never been officially told what happened. It was only after numerous telephone calls, each striving to access the information that they needed,

*James Ashley*

*Paul Whitehouse*

that they finally established that the dead man was their son and brother.

To make a tragic situation even worse, a few hours after stumbling on the news of Jimmy's death, the family were to hear on television Chief Constable Paul Whitehouse publicly casting false aspersions on Jimmy's character and insisting that his officers had acted properly.

The family made a referral to the Police Complaints Authority. It was after that complaint was made that the PCA commissioned reports into what had happened. Barbara Wilding, then Assistant Chief Constable of Hampshire Police, was asked to produce a report into the Chief Constable's involvement in what happened. Those reports were produced and delivered to the PCA, which, following its normal procedures, issued letters accepting the adequacy of the reports. Yet neither report has ever been published and neither report has been exposed to public scrutiny.

The information in the reports has become known only because there were leaks to the press, specifically to The Guardian which published a detailed article in 2001. I draw on much of the information in the leaked articles for my comments.

It is a matter of importance, for the record, that, to the best of my knowledge, nothing in the reports has been denied. The Wilding Report found a complete failure of corporate duty by Sussex police. The Hampshire inquiry concluded that three police officers lied about intelligence in order to persuade Deputy Chief Constable Mark Jordan to authorise the raid. The report found that the raid was 'authorised on intelligence that was not merely exaggerated, it was determinably false... there was a plan to deceive and the evidence concocted'.

That is absolutely damning.

The report also showed that the guidelines on firearms put together by the Association of Chief Police Officers were breached. Experts on firearms and the law told Kent police that even if the intelligence had been correct, the firearms should not have been authorised.

The Chief Constable was castigated. Sir John Hoddinott concluded that Paul Whitehouse, the then Chief Constable, 'wilfully failed to tell the truth as he knew it, he did so without reasonable excuse or justification and what he published and said was misleading'.

Sir John found evidence against Deputy Chief Constable Mark Jordan. That included criminal misfeasance and neglect of duty, discreditable conduct and aiding and abetting the Chief Constable's false statements. There was suggested evidence of collusion between some or all of the chief officers and an arguable case of attempting to pervert the course of justice.

These statements were contained in those investigation reports. The reports have been kept secret - apart from the leaks made to the press - and have never been available for public scrutiny. After four years, it is reasonable to ask what action has been taken in the face of such gross abuses.

I note that there are a number of players in the complaints system for the police, which has relevance when we consider that four years have passed. Those players are the Police Complaints Authority, the Crown Prosecution Service, the Sussex police authority and others. In considering the comments that I am about to make, I ask my Right Honourable Friend the Minister to consider what the role of those key players should have been and where the dereliction of duty lay.

The CPS refused to prosecute senior officers. In May 2001, the presiding judge halted the Old Bailey trial of the police officer who shot James Ashley dead. At a separate trial in Wolverhampton the same month, the officers who planned the raid were acquitted when the CPS offered no evidence, alleging that the depth of corporate failure was too great to make any individual responsible. Two of the officers involved were promoted with backdated pay increases - an insult to the memory of James Ashley and an absolute affront to his bereaved family.

Deputy Chief Constable Mark Jordan was suspended on full pay for nearly three years before being retired permanently on ill-health grounds with a full retirement pension at the age of forty-three. That enabled him to escape disciplinary procedures, yet on 21 March 1998, during the debate on the Home Affairs Committee inquiry into police complaints in the aftermath of anger about the consequences of the Hillsborough tragedy, the House was promised that the police would no longer be able to evade disciplinary action in that way. That promise was given to the House in March 1998, yet four years afterwards apparently nothing has happened.

Indeed, the definitive action has been the resignation of Chief Constable Paul Whitehouse in June 2001. That followed an intervention by my Right Honourable Friend the Home Secretary. I praise the Home Secretary for his resolute action. His was the first clear action from the Home Office that led to the police having to face up to the consequences of what they had done. In the days that followed the Home Secretary's statement, Paul Whitehouse started to criticise the Home Secretary and queried the legitimacy of his statement, but the result was obtained, and Paul Whitehouse, the Chief Constable at the time of the shooting, resigned.

During the past two months disciplinary charges have been filed against three police officers. I presume that the hearings that relate to the disciplinary charges will be internal, not a matter for public scrutiny.

What should happen now? It is self-evident that the criminal justice system has failed the Ashleys. I call for the immediate publication of the Hoddinott and Wilding reports and for a full public inquiry into the events that led up to the shooting of James Ashley and in its aftermath, including the handling of the complaints.

Today, by a great coincidence, I have seen a report submitted by Sussex Police Authority that says that the Police Inspectorate has carried out an investigation, twenty-six recommendations about changes in the way that Sussex Police operate have been made and that many of them have been implemented. However, having read that report, I still find it impossible to ascertain whether all those recommendations have been implemented. Indeed, none of them refers to the need for public scrutiny of what happened on the early morning when James Ashley was shot dead. Nothing in the report tells us how we should overhaul the police complaints system.

In a letter to me dated 27 June 2001, Sir Alistair Graham, the chairman of the Complaints Authority, stated: "it is not possible to let you have a copy of Barbara Wilding's and John Hoddinott's reports as section 80 of the Police Act 1996 specifically debars us from doing this except in special circumstances."

After four years of non-action, I plead those special circumstances. I specifically reject the explanation passed to me by my Right Honourable Friend the Minister of 8 January 2002 when I was informed that the reports could not be made public because the Sussex Police Authority would not agree to it. It cannot be acceptable for a Police

> Authority that is in the dock itself to veto action of such great public importance. I do not intend to shoot the messenger, but I castigate the ruling of the Police Authority. *(Hansard excerpt concludes)*

This sad episode coincided with one of the worst periods in Sussex Police's history and it was not until the appointment of Ken Jones, now Sir Ken Jones, as Chief Constable, that better days returned to the force.

# CHAPTER 4

## Internal impact factors

When police misconduct or corruption is talked about, consideration needs to be given to the issue of police culture. This subject has evoked considerable academic debate amongst sociologists over the years, in particular PAJ Waddington, Robert Reiner and Nick Manning, and is often focused upon as a negative concept. Every organisation develops its own culture so why is police culture perceived as being different to any other and why is it seen in such a negative way in many quarters?

There has been much discussion over what it consists of. Reiner has described it as 'the values, norms, perspectives and craft rules which inform police conduct'. However, a different definition comes from Manning who defines it as 'accepted practices, rules, and principles of conduct that are situationally applied, and generalised rationales and beliefs'. Although these definitions don't appear too different at first glance, there is, in fact, a clear distinction between the two that must be made. Manning stresses that such principles of conduct are 'situationally applied', which of course suggests that 'police culture' is not always necessarily influential to an officer's conduct.

Some officers can and do hold a certain level of professionalism when taking to the streets and any values which may corrupt such professionalism remain behind closed doors in the company of their colleagues only. Yet Reiner's definition suggests that the police culture remains with the police officer when they take to the streets. He/she then enforces the informal rules which have been established with their fellow colleagues, which generalises that all police officers act in accordance with the 'police culture'. However, what must be taken from both definitions is that there is reason to suggest that there is a network of a shared set of norms and values within police forces which could potentially affect how they operate in a working environment. Is this significantly different to any other organisation? Or is this more about a focus on policing, through academia more interested in justifying criticism of the police and how they act in carrying out law enforcement?

What must be stressed is that there is also a distinction between the terms 'police culture', or 'cop culture', as it's sometimes referred to, and 'canteen culture', which is another concept which crops up time and again in countless criminology texts. 'Canteen culture', as mentioned by Waddington, is understood to be the norms and values held by police officers whilst off-duty, whereas 'police culture' is more about the norms and values which are expressed during their occupational lives. There is another view that also makes this a key point by explaining that there is a common tendency to assume that what police choose to say and how they choose to act when off duty is not only indicative of how police officers think, but also how they act in public. Waddington, however, claims that this is not the case, all the time. The way officers act and the views they hold whilst off duty, whether in the pub with friends or work colleagues, is but a 'safety valve to release the pressures of the realities of life as a police officer'. Such an argument claims that, in experiencing somewhat controversial views outside the working sphere, a person is opened up to new perspectives which sociologists such as Waddington would argue helps to avoid them being over-exposed to a particular ideology which could then influence the way in which they carry out their duties. However, what also must be considered is just how valid Waddington's argument actually is. Yes, of course, in some instances, exposure to different attitudes and values can be beneficial to an officer, in terms of becoming more aware of potential new threats, but there are also some officers who would then, due to any extreme views to which they may have been subjected, target an individual or a group of people because of the stereotypes attached to such persons and not because of genuine suspicion. Therefore, this has a valid place, if accepted, in helping to understand why some officers become involved in misconduct and corruption.

Reiner claims that 'police culture' has many characteristics, and 'suspicion' is just one of them. Suspicion is an absolute necessity in the police service as it is suspicion that helps the police prevent crimes from occurring, as well as investigating those committed. Therefore, in this view, everyday working experiences encourage officers to generalise people with labels, whether or not this is a legitimate way to suspect possible offenders. There are those who are prepared to argue that there is a strong link between suspicion and ethnicity, with ethnic minorities suspected of engaging in criminal activity more than people of white ethnic origin. When considering statistics relating to police 'stop and search', some place great emphasis upon this issue. In interpreting the results of 'stop and search' practices, there is always a focus on the proportion of BAME people subjected to this power as opposed to those described as being white. This perception, however, doesn't end with the police. It has been suggested that it branches out into other areas of the criminal justice system, such as the prison service.

Some academics and other individuals have attempted to suggest that racial prejudice is a problematic characteristic of a 'police culture', in terms of the impact it has on police and community relations. The same commentators often cite the *Macpherson Report* into the Stephen Lawrence case, as justification for their claims. As we all know, that report stated that the police were 'institutionally racist', after discovering that police were ignoring evidence crucial to the investigation. In addition, it was claimed they were displaying either conscious or unconscious discrimination in the interviewing process of suspects, by suggesting it was a black-on-black crime, despite

Lawrence's friend Duwayne Brooks, an eyewitness, being adamant that it was a racially-motivated murder. Despite the findings of the report, and the provisions set out to try and avoid the recurrence of racial controversy within the police, it is a fact, even allowing for recent advances, that minority ethnic recruitment remains low and there are continuing problems in terms of police relations with ethnic minorities. Some still believed that, even after the *Macpherson Report*, institutional racism was still rife in police recruitment centres. Four years after the report was published, a BBC documentary titled *The Secret Policeman* focused on the police recruitment centre, Bruche, located just outside Warrington. After the documentary went public, the centre was closed so as to not further damage the reputation of the police. New police training systems were also introduced nationwide to try and expel racism from the police force.

Some believe that the issue of how officers socialise is greatly significant. It is inevitable that within any existing so-called 'police culture', there is a degree of solidarity, and it is this element which, although reinforced in numerous police forces, is an aspect initially developed between candidates during the recruitment stages. Due to the intense nature of the job, including the long hours which officers work, the intensity of the work and the expectation of being the ones to 'fight the good fight' on behalf of society, officers are encouraged to bond strongly and learn to rely on one another. As such, they tend to develop an 'us against them' attitude. This can, in some situations, lead to officers making pacts in which they agree not to 'grass' on fellow officers for any bad behaviour that they see whilst on duty. This has been referred to as 'The Blue Code of Silence'. Just like any other so-called subculture, in order to ensure co-operation and commitment to the 'Blue Code', a value system can be implemented which makes 'police culture' something like a family structure, in which members of the system receive emotional support and security from other officers. Several police departments worldwide have been found to have followed this 'Blue Code'. Probably the most notable was a New York police department which the Mollen Commission reported as covering up infringements by their officers. If an officer were to break the Code, then his/her reputation, and essentially his/her career too, would be ruined as he/she would be ostracised and labelled a whistleblower. Thus, it is the threat of this tarnished reputation that encourages the officer to obey the unwritten rules in some cases. Of course, one of the main reasons for the development of the Police Code of Ethics was to change this and to place a requirement on officers to confront misconduct and if sufficiently serious, formally report it.

Accusations of excessive force by the police are far from uncommon. It is the use of excessive force which writers such as Manning claim is a perfect example of the negative aspects of 'police culture' and how it can have a detrimental impact on the way officers carry out their duties. However, excessive force is not detected in all cases. Victims of what is often referred to as police brutality may feel that the odds are stacked against them in making a complaint to an officer's superiors. Therefore, they are reluctant to do so and may feel that, even if a complaint results in a court case or a misconduct hearing, the judge and jury or a tribunal would overlook excessive force. This is because their perceived perspective could be that the victim shouldn't have got him/herself in a position in which the use of force was needed in the first place and therefore the consequences were deserved.

Yet with that said, there are, of course, examples where individuals don't deserve such treatment and thus the police force as a whole has come under criticism, despite it being a minority of officers who participate in such excessive violence. For example, a police constable, Simon Harwood, was charged with the manslaughter of Ian Tomlinson during the G20 protests in 2009. Tomlinson was finding another route home after his usual route was blocked by the protests, when he was struck by PC Harwood with a baton and then pushed to the ground. Tomlinson fatally collapsed and an autopsy revealed the cause of death was a heart attack, in which the actions of PC Harwood were no doubt a triggering factor. He was acquitted of manslaughter, which some will have seen as only strengthening the argument that the courts may be sympathetic to the police when the question of reasonable/excessive force is raised.

However, it must be stressed that many police forces do have provisions in place to deal with complaints of unacceptable behaviour by their officers in which enquiries will be carried out and, if found guilty, the officer in question may be dealt with in accordance with the procedures already described. Also, as in the case of PC Harwood, they can face criminal prosecution or at the very least, a civil hearing if the complainant sues for damages.

There clearly must have been cases where police officers got away with these kinds of infringements. How have these happened? Arguably it is again linked to 'The Blue Code of Silence'. As already mentioned, some officers claim ignorance of any wrongdoings of their colleagues and in some cases, may even provide false accounts to support them. Relating back to the so-called 'Blue Code', not supporting a colleague in this way could lead to an officer being shunned and sometimes even harassed to the point of leaving the force, as they aren't assisting their 'family' members, in effect betraying their own kind.

This seeming pre-occupation with the perceived 'police culture' may be due to the negative impact it can and sometimes does have on society when things go wrong and officers are guilty of misconduct. As previously stated, the police hold a massively important role in society as a visible symbol of law and order and are granted various powers, such as those which enable them to arrest members of the public who are often a very real threat to the rest of society. Although most officers do operate in a reasonable manner, it is generally the actions of the minority which on occasions can lead the public to believe that all officers are bigoted and aggressive. Such generalisations can lead to mistrust of the police, and tensions begin to occur between police and public. You only need to look at the summer riots of 2011, which began with an officer shooting dead a suspect, to see just how damaging poor police community relations can be to the police's image as a social institution.

The concept of the so-called 'Police Canteen Culture' is critical as it is often used to describe a perceived influence on the behaviour of groups of officers. The 'canteen' is a collective term for groups of police officers to discuss problems encountered in operational policing scenarios. It is seen as operating in the background and something which is not clearly evident, even to officers themselves, and is an almost invisible phenomenon. It is often seen as negative, with it being referred to by some as responsible for poor police behaviour and potential corruption. This is somewhat different from 'the street' where actions undertaken by officers are witnessed by their peers and the public, of course.

The often-held belief that police officers possess a distinctive occupational sub-culture lies at the heart of a considerable amount of academic debate. Much of this is linked to the fact that police officers operate within an arena where there is a high degree of discretion in terms of law enforcement. Some therefore believe that this discretion can be influenced by inherent beliefs developed through the so-called 'canteen' culture. Again, it is often seen as negative, responsible for injustices and a barrier to enlightened change.

Speaking practically, a considerable amount of informal debriefing took place in canteens and police bars. Many believe that such discussions ensured that officers could offload some of the difficult and very unpleasant tasks they had dealt with, or the issues they had encountered. Police bars are now a thing of the past, having been closed over the years to develop additional office space. Similarly, canteens have also closed and very few continue to operate, save those run as franchises at various police headquarters. This is very important because I very much doubt that the so-called 'canteen' culture no longer exists and therefore there must still be a means by which officers continue to discuss operational experiences and their beliefs.

In considering police behaviour, the Stephen Lawrence case is useful because it has huge associations, not only with cultural issues within the police, but also with allegations of police corruption and wrongdoing. To provide context, the case is summarised here through a timeline and coverage of some of the issues that were widely reported in the media and elsewhere. The case shows just how easily a poorly run police investigation can, in certain circumstances, escalate into something completely different. This, in the Lawrence case, raised a significant number of allegations which, even to this day, have been neither proven nor indeed disproven and have therefore left a nasty taste in the mouth. Some commentators have described the case as a turning point in UK policing. I am not sure this is necessarily so. It is, however, the case that, far from addressing some issues in policing that needed addressing, it has served to instil a fear within senior levels of the police. To some extent, the organisation now seems hamstrung, to the extent where occasionally, it fails to tackle some problems robustly for fear of criticism or worse.

Stephen Lawrence was a black British teenager from Plumstead, south east London, who was murdered in a racially-motivated attack while waiting for a bus in Well Hall, Eltham, on the evening of 22 April 1993. With him was Duwayne Brooks, himself arrested several days later after an anti-racist march outside the British National Party's headquarters. However, a judge dismissed this charge.

On 23 April, police began to receive the same names repeatedly, identifying the killers. In May and June, after the initial investigation, five suspects - Neil and Jamie Acourt, David Norris, Gary Dobson and Luke Knight - were arrested but not charged, as the police were still convinced it was a black-on-black murder, despite Duwayne insisting the attack was racially motivated. Duwayne also identified Neil Acourt and Luke Knight as two of the killers and they were then charged. However, the CPS dropped the case in July, saying Duwayne's ID evidence was unreliable. In 1994, Stephen's parents, Doreen and Neville, launched a private prosecution against Dobson, Knight and Neil Acourt. However, once again, the case collapsed when the judge ruled that Duwayne's ID evidence was inadmissible.

In March 1997, after the *Daily Mail* had named the five men as responsible for the murder, inviting them to sue if the claim is wrong (they didn't!), Kent Police launched an investigation into police conduct, which nine months later highlighted 'significant weaknesses, omissions and lost opportunities' but said the Met had been institutionally incompetent, rather than institutionally racist. This just goes to demonstrate how if things go badly wrong, there is a strong likelihood of things escalating out of control, to the point where the fundamental problems, if not overlooked, have less emphasis placed upon them. In this case, I would argue that the main problem was a lack of investigative ability on the part of those leading the original investigation. Whether institutional racism underpinned this is the key issue and I am not sure it has ever been proven one way or the other.

On 31 July 1997, Home Secretary Jack Straw ordered a public enquiry, to be conducted by Sir William Macpherson and officially titled *The Inquiry Into The Matters Arising From The Death of Stephen Lawrence*, and published as the *Macpherson Report*. The report, produced in February 1999, estimated that it had taken 'more than 100,000 pages of reports, statements, and other written or printed documents' and also concluded that the original Met investigation had been incompetent, with some officers committing fundamental errors, including failing to give first aid when they reached the scene; failing to follow obvious leads during their investigation; and failing to arrest suspects. The report found that there had been a failure of leadership by senior Met officers and that recommendations in the 1981 *Scarman Report*, compiled following race-related riots in Brixton and Toxteth, had been ignored. Almost unbelievably, Detective Superintendent Brian Weeden said, during the inquiry, that mistakes had been made in the murder investigation, including an incredible admission that he hadn't known he could have arrested the suspects four days after the killing, simply on reasonable suspicion, a basic point of criminal law.

The report also found that the Metropolitan Police was institutionally racist. Seventy recommendations for reform, covering both policing and criminal law, were made. These proposals included abolishing the double jeopardy rule and criminalising racist statements made in private. Macpherson also called for reform in the British Civil Service, local governments, the National Health Service, schools, and the judicial system, to address issues of institutional racism.

In 1997, Lawrence's family had registered a formal complaint with the then Police Complaints Authority (PCA), which in 1999 exonerated case officers of allegations of racism. The officers, all now retired, were Detective Superintendent Ian Crampton, in charge for the first three days after the murder, Detective Superintendent Brian Weeden, who took over as Senior Investigating Officer, Detective Chief Superintendent William Ilsley, who oversaw them, and Detective Inspector Ben Bullock. Only DI Bullock, second in command of the investigation, was ordered to face disciplinary charges for neglect of duty. Four other officers retired before the investigation into the complaint concluded.

Bullock was later found guilty of a failure to properly brief officers and failure to fully investigate an anonymous letter sent

*Stephen Lawrence*

*Brian Weeden*

*Ben Bullock*

*Gary Dobson*

*David Norris*

to police, but he was acquitted of eleven other charges. He retired the day after his punishment was announced, so it amounted to a mere caution. Neville Lawrence, Stephen's father, criticised the punishment, saying that Bullock was 'guilty on all counts'. However, a spokesperson for the Metropolitan Police Federation stated that Bullock had been 'largely vindicated' in the proceedings.

On 10 March 2006, the Metropolitan Police announced that it would pay Duwayne Brooks £100,000 as compensation for the manner in which police had handled his complaints about their actions toward him after the murder.

On 25 July 2006, the Independent Police Complaints Commission IPCC) announced that it had asked the Met to look into alleged claims of police corruption that may have helped hide Stephen's killers.

On 17 December 2009, IPCC investigators and officers from the Met's Directorate of Professional Standards arrested a former police constable and a serving member of the Metropolitan Police staff, on suspicion of attempting to pervert the course of justice by allegedly withholding evidence from the original murder inquiry, the Kent investigation and the Macpherson Inquiry. Dr Richard Stone, who sat on the Macpherson Inquiry, commented that the panel had felt that there was 'a large amount of information that the police were either not processing or were suppressing' and 'a strong smell of corruption'. Baroness Ros Howells, patron of the Stephen Lawrence Charitable Trust, agreed: 'Lots of people said they gave the police evidence which was never produced.' On 1 March 2010, the IPCC announced that no further action would be taken against the two men and they were released.

On 18 May 2011, after a further review, it was announced that two of the original suspects, Gary Dobson and David Norris, were to stand trial for the murder in the light of new evidence. At the same time, it was disclosed that Dobson's original acquittal had been quashed by the Court of Appeal, allowing a retrial to take place. Such a course of action had only become possible following the 2005 change in the law, although Dobson was not the first person to be retried for murder as a result. On 3 January 2012, Dobson and Norris were found guilty of Lawrence's murder. The pair were juveniles at the time of the crime and so were sentenced to detention at Her Majesty's Pleasure, equivalent to a life sentence for an adult, with minimum terms of fifteen years two months and fourteen years three months respectively for what the judge described as a 'terrible and evil crime'.

Following the convictions, further inquiries by both Scotland Yard and the IPCC ruled that there was no new evidence to warrant further investigation.

In the years after Dobson and Norris were sentenced, the case regained prominence when further concerns of corrupt police conduct during the original case handling surfaced in the media. As if all of this were not enough, it was also claimed publicly that the police spied on the Lawrence family, alleging that the Met was apparently fearful of the reputational and social consequences of its own botched murder investigation.

Such claims had surfaced before, and been investigated in 2006, but were reignited in June 2013, when an interview with Peter Francis, a former undercover police officer, was published in *The Guardian*. In the interview, Francis stated that, while he was working undercover within an anti-racist campaign group in the mid-1990s, he was constantly pressured by superiors to 'smear' the credibility of Lawrence's family so as to end the campaign for a better investigation into Stephen's death.

The Met launched Operation Herne, led by Chief Constable Mick Creedon, which investigated Peter Francis' allegations and, in March 2014, reported it had found no evidence to back up his claims. Prime Minister David Cameron said he was 'deeply worried about the reports'. In the meantime, following Francis' interview in 2013, after discussions with Doreen Lawrence, Home Secretary Theresa May commissioned Mark Ellison QC to review Scotland Yard's investigations into alleged police corruption, pledging to be 'ruthless about purging corruption from the police'. May asked Ellison to identify specific cases where undercover police operations had been used and where these may have led to potential miscarriages of justice. One of these is well documented and involved twenty-nine climate change protesters who had their convictions quashed because the case against them involved undisclosed information gathered by undercover police officer Mark Kennedy. In the words of the prosecutor, it was a 'catastrophic failure of disclosure'. This case will feature again within this book.

On 6 March 2014, Mark Ellison's report, titled *The Stephen Lawrence Independent Review*, was presented to Parliament. Sir Bernard Hogan-Howe, Commissioner of the Metropolitan Police at that time, said the report, which prompted an inquiry into undercover policing, was 'devastating'. Ellison's report also showed that there was substantial evidence linking an alleged corrupt police officer with involvement in the murder of private investigator Daniel Morgan in 1987, when Morgan, it was alleged, was close to exposing police corruption.

In 2015, under the direction of the now IOPC, the National Crime Agency also began to investigate claims of corruption in the Lawrence case, prompted by the 2014 Ellison review. The multi-million-pound investigation into why officers in charge of the first Met investigation into Stephen's murder did not make arrests for two weeks, despite officers repeatedly being given the names of suspects, took five years and investigated whether the five Lawrence murder suspects were shielded because of corruption and who, if anyone, in Scotland Yard was involved.

On 3 November 2020, it was announced that the report arising out of the investigation had been referred to the Crown Prosecution Service who were asked to consider if four senior officers committed misconduct in public office. All four strenuously denied committing any offences, with supporters claiming they were victims of a 'politically motivated witch hunt'. They were interviewed under caution, which does not imply guilt. The offence of misconduct in public office, effectively breach of duty, carries a maximum sentence of life imprisonment. It remains to be seen whether there is any evidence to suggest the officers acted corruptly.

In addition to all this, considerable media coverage since Stephen's murder has consistently explored alleged relationships between Met police officers and Clifford Norris, the father of David Norris, convicted in 2012 of Stephen's murder.

Such connections were well-known within Clifford's extended family, who made claims that he used a network of corrupt officers to protect himself and his close relations from justice. Family members stated openly that the area from Bermondsey to Greenwich was known as the cocaine mile and that Clifford, who lived on the south London and Kent border in Chislehurst and was a known drug smuggler, 'had the old bill in his pocket in every nick'. Naomi Smith, closely related to the Norris family by marriage, stated that she knew Clifford was a police informant and recalled a local individual from south London saying, 'There goes Clifford, giving up bods', a slang term meaning giving up fellow criminals to the police. This could be important because one of the things that the police should test out when recruiting and using informants is their motivation. It is a fact that some informants do 'shop' other criminals to remove competition.

The 2012 conviction of David Norris, nineteen years after Stephen's murder, gave Naomi and her daughter Victoria the confidence to come forward to make their claims of police corruption. In *The Guardian,* they alleged that Clifford had used corrupt officers to thwart a previous murder inquiry in 1989, four years before Stephen was killed. They said that Tony Smith, Naomi's son and Victoria's brother, stabbed Alex Norris,

Clifford's brother, in a fight in a pub called the Old Manor in Deptford in May 1989, after which Alex shot Tony dead. There were allegedly twenty people in the pub but apparently nobody witnessed anything! The Smith family claimed that potential witnesses were intimidated by Alex. After Alex quickly became a suspect, Clifford used his influence to continue to intimidate witnesses. No one was ever charged, and Vanessa and Naomi alleged sensitive information they gave the police ended up being passed to Norris.

It was also reported that Christine Clapp-Smith, Clifford's sister-in-law, had, it was alleged, an affair with Clifford and sold drugs for him. Two days after the pub shooting, she visited Naomi and Victoria and said she would go to the police. Naomi told the police they were about to get a new witness to Alex's involvement. However, the next morning, the Smith family claimed that Christine was visited at her home and told at gunpoint she would be killed unless she kept silent.

Alex Norris was arrested on suspicion of Tony Smith's murder, but the case against him was dropped. He was later jailed for drug offences following an investigation by HM Customs and Excise.

The Smiths also said that Clifford Norris similarly used his influence with the police after Stephen's murder. Victoria alleged that, if the police had done their job properly after her brother was killed, then Doreen Lawrence would not have gone through what she had to endure. She claimed the police left Clifford Norris at large and untouched to use his influence upon them. She also stated in 2014 that the Met was told of their claims about the Norrises and the corrupt links to police officers but that the Met did not seem interested. Whilst they told officers everything, they were not pushed or pressed on any of the information they provided on Clifford Norris.

The extent of Clifford Norris' reach into the Met Police has long been a matter of controversy, with some former Met officers claiming it went back as far as 1978. The claims made regarding the Tony Smith case were only part of several allegations regarding the suggested influence of the Norris family over the Metropolitan Police, particularly in relation to Stephen's murder. A former associate of Clifford's alleged he had bribed officers and claimed he could name a specific premises where payments were made. This individual said they offered this information to the Met but that it was not acted upon. Connections between Norris and the police were also suspected by a former senior investigator in HM Customs and Excise, who feared corruption was blocking the agency's efforts to look into his drug-smuggling operations.

The potential fear the Norris family was able to exert on a murder investigation was noted by the Macpherson Inquiry. Macpherson described Clifford Norris as 'evil' and a 'malign influence'. The report said that, in the Lawrence case, 'officers were aware of threats coming from him which were discouraging the witnesses who were so desperately sought'. Another Met officer, David Coles, was seen meeting Clifford Norris and exchanging packages, the Macpherson Inquiry heard.

Former Met Police Deputy Assistant Commissioner John Grieve, who led the third investigation into the Lawrence case, said in 2006, 'During the investigation I led, we feared corruption might have played a part in the failure of the first investigation.'

Clive Driscoll, a former Met DCI who, in 2012, helped secure the two convictions for Stephen's murder, including that of David Norris, told *The Guardian* that examining how Clifford Norris had operated after the Smith killing may help investigators hoping to bring new charges in the Lawrence murder. 'It is important because there are nominals [people of interest to the police] in the Tony Smith murder that are also nominals in Stephen's murder. It gives an insight into criminal activity in that area and how they operated, which may be relevant to both cases. It's always intrigued me that anyone would think that [the Norrises] would not try to influence the investigation. If they had the links already, common sense tells me they would use them.'

After Stephen's murder, it was claimed that Clifford returned from a self-imposed exile overseas to threaten a witness, Stacey Benefield, who was alleged to have been stabbed by David Norris with a sword, the Macpherson Inquiry heard. The threats against Benefield were made three days after he had picked David Norris out of an identity parade as the person who had allegedly attacked him. Clifford Norris and an associate even knew in what room the identity parade had taken place, according to the *Macpherson Report* and witness statements from Benefield.

In a 2006 interview with the *Observer*, Clifford Norris denied he had ever had corrupt associations with police officers. He stated, 'I never became involved with underhand dealings or giving money to coppers. Never did I give the police any money or a retainer to get them on the payroll. I don't know any bent coppers.' Norris admitted, however, that he was aware of corruption between officers and other criminals in the period around Stephen's murder.

In a BBC investigation, *The Boys Who Killed Stephen Lawrence,* shown on 26 July 2006, Neil Putnam, a former corrupt police detective turned whistleblower, told the BBC that Clifford was paying the murder inquiry's Detective Sergeant John Davidson to obstruct the case and protect the suspects. 'Davidson told me he was looking after Norris and that to me meant he was protecting him, protecting his family against arrest and any conviction,' Putnam said. Davidson denied any such corruption. Following the documentary, the Met opened a special incident room to field calls from the public. However the IPCC later stated that the claims made in the programme were unfounded. It would take until 2014 for the official report ordered by Theresa May to find there was 'reason to suspect' Davidson of corruption in the Lawrence case, some twelve years after the allegations first surfaced.

Stephen's parents, Doreen and Neville, had long suspected that Clifford Norris and police corruption played a part in their son's killers evading justice for almost two decades. Doreen is reported as saying in *The Guardian* that what this showed was that practically everybody seems to have known about this alleged corrupt relationship. It appeared to have been an open secret. It therefore beggars belief that those investigating corruption in the police did not know. She went on to say, 'I don't accept that they didn't know, especially when it now appears that the police refused to act upon this information when it was handed to them on a plate. I thought that after twenty-five years I could no longer be shocked by the conduct of the Metropolitan Police. However, if it is true that they did this, my sense of outrage will have risen to new heights and I will want immediate answers from them as to why it happened and why I was not told.'

So what does the Stephen Lawrence case achieve in terms of improving our understanding of police corruption? Well, firstly, we need to ensure that we do not lose our focus as regards what a poorly conducted initial investigation it was. It is as clear as day that opportunities were missed right in the initial stages. There was the chance to arrest the main suspects in the case at the very beginning. For any senior investigator to suggest that there was insufficient evidence or suspicion to justify arrests is tantamount to stupidity. Those suspects should have been arrested very early on and searches of premises at that time would have undoubtedly led to the retrieval of evidence which would have led to potential convictions.

The key question therefore becomes simply this. Was this failing triggered through ineptitude or was there something more sinister at play? Indeed, could it have been a combination of both? Of course, with the passage of time, we will probably never get to the bottom of it. Suffice it to say, the conclusion is entirely unsatisfactory because, to date, not all those responsible for Stephen Lawrence's murder have been brought to justice. The fact that his murder was racially-motivated is no longer in any doubt and should not have been, right from the outset. It is therefore a travesty that the case remains, to a large extent, unresolved to this day.

Considering the issue of police corruption and misconduct linked to police culture, it's the case that culture within the police is probably not much different to that experienced, for instance, within the military. This is because, similar to the armed services, the police service has relied on a high level of discipline, albeit this is far less the case these days. Such organisations develop a certain *esprit de corps*. Seen in a positive light, this can be a good thing because strong teams tend to perform well. On the other hand, as acknowledged previously, it can also lead to a potential closing of ranks and thus becomes a hindrance to dealing with those officers guilty of misconduct or corruption. It is therefore this latter aspect which is the potential danger area. Fortunately, I have never witnessed this personally but that does not mean it hasn't happened. I am not naïve enough to believe that such antics and behaviour have not gone on in the past and still do so today. That is a fact of life. However, we do need to tighten up existing mechanisms and develop new ones to lessen the likelihood of it happening.

Jealousy is an awful thing in normal circumstances. However, it can be a major contributor to a somewhat insidious and yet almost hidden form of corruption in policing. What I am about to describe is by no means unique to the police service. However, I have witnessed its effects both at first hand and in terms of the impact on others. Some of what I will refer to featured in my first book *My Way*. However, I intend to build on this in terms of the impact of what I perceive to be jealousy.

Within the police service, it is a fact that operational competence, even excellence, is a much-envied quality. Those individuals who can point to consistently high performance, whether as a senior investigator, for example, or as an operational commander, will inevitably find things significantly easier, in terms of management and leadership, than those who do not possess such qualities. I know this because like every senior police leader, I served first of all in the junior ranks and I recall those senior officers whom I attempted to emulate because of their operational capabilities.

Additionally, policing is a results-driven business. In order to achieve success as a senior leader, whether this is as a senior investigator leading murder teams or as a divisional or departmental commander, success very much depends on the efforts of those who work for you. Some leaders seem to forget this on occasions. To bring the best out of a team and in an effort to bring about excellent performance, these teams need to be led and managed. This is easier to achieve if those working for you recognise that you have been there and done it.

The issue of jealousy can manifest itself in several ways. Firstly, there is absolutely no doubt that promotions and other forms of advancement can be delayed because of jealousy. Individuals in positions of power can influence those at a similar level or higher in a negative way, to the detriment of others. In many respects, jealousy can almost go hand in glove with nepotism, which I have discussed previously. The case of Detective Superintendent Tony Lundy will be covered later. At this point, it is enough to say that a potential witch hunt against him led to him being targeted for alleged wrongdoing in relation to the handling of informants. Of course, there are always two sides to most things and Tony Lundy's case was no exception.

My own promotion to chief superintendent was delayed because of adverse opinions provided to senior management by some of my peers. My then Assistant Chief Constable told me as much on a visit to see me when I was undertaking the role of Divisional Commander for Brighton and Hove. He told me that my performance in the role had allayed previous perceptions he had had of me, provided to him by unnamed sources. It is therefore clear that the jaundiced views of some regarding the methods of others can be negatively portrayed to those in very senior positions and can affect careers.

There is ample evidence to suggest that jealousy is and always has been alive and well, within the police service. My overall point therefore is simply this. Such behaviour is a form of corruption and is bred easily if cliques are allowed to develop within the organisation. Careers can be stunted or damaged.

Another example of such behaviour can occur when those in senior positions fear the capabilities of those working for them. In other words, knowledge and experience are power. After my retirement as a police officer, I became the Intelligence Manager within the South East Regional Organised Crime Unit (ROCU), employed as a senior member of police staff/civilian. I openly admit that I was often frustrated as I was unable to influence things to the extent that my previous seniority had allowed. However, my experience meant that I was still quite capable of identifying issues that needed addressing and I regularly made this known to those working at levels above me.

My opinions were not always welcome, despite my knowledge levels and previous experience. Such attitudes are disappointing because good policing relies on good teamwork. To me, it never mattered who had the best ideas, regardless of the levels they may have occupied within the organisation. It is not a sign of weakness to accept that an individual may have better ideas than somebody more senior. Seniority is not always necessarily about knowledge. It is likely to be the case that an individual not afraid to come forward with their ideas is a sign of good leadership by their managers, through encouraging members of their team to do exactly that.

# CHAPTER 5

## What are the risks and how do we mitigate these?

The list of constant and variable factors in police corruption illustrates two quite simple but important points. The first is that the very nature of policing means that the potential for corruption is always present. This is because the nature of policing means that officers come into contact with criminal elements and often have to operate in environments which mean that some will be vulnerable to corruption. Second, and to reinforce an earlier point, tackling corruption is by no means straightforward, with the range of factors involved needing to be matched by a wide range of preventive and investigative measures.

One of the key concepts regarding police wrongdoing is the issue of so-called 'noble cause' corruption and the risks associated with this and how to prevent it. In a nutshell, the term 'noble cause' corruption concerns the extent to which it is reasonable to use 'dirty' or unconventional means to achieve 'noble' ends. Debates around this question are often summarised as the 'Dirty Harry' problem, from the Clint Eastwood movies in which the protagonist, a San Francisco detective, uses increasingly unconventional and unethical/illegal means in his attempts to fight serious crime, especially cases involving extreme violence. What these movies, novels by various crime fiction writers and other films and TV shows ask of us is whether we side with 'justice' and with the cop trying to deal with the most vicious and violent offenders?

Therefore, the issue of 'noble cause' corruption is important for several reasons. First, there is evidence that matters such as 'perverting the course of justice' rank high among the public as alluded to in the IPCC report of 2011 entitled *Corruption In The Police Service Of England And Wales*. Secondly, it appears that allegations about irregularities in relation to evidence and perjury are among the more frequent complaints from the public about police conduct. The same IPCC report recognises this as an issue. Finally, there are suggestions that aspects of police culture, including the emphasis on performance targets, increase the pressure. As a quote by a CID officer, recorded in a report completed by Her Majesty's Inspectorate of Constabulary (HMIC) in June 1999, *Police Integrity England, Wales And Northern Ireland Securing And Maintaining Public Confidence*, there is pressure on officers to 'operate at the edge of the ethical'.

So, is there a simple answer to the 'Dirty Harry' problem? Some would say it is a straightforward 'yes', and that dirty means can never justify so-called 'noble' ends. In fact, there are few who would openly disagree. However, it is clear from studies of policing in practice that some officers, and occasionally some in supervisory or managerial roles, either deliberately or through turning a blind eye, endorse such conduct.

That this is the case would come as no surprise to some academics. A number have argued that this is an area of ethical complexity and that, in reality, it is a problem to which there is no easy resolution for the police. I have already referred to the problem of competition within policing and that this has a huge bearing on this issue. Additionally, and again arguably, it needs to be recognised not only that 'Dirty Harry' dilemmas are almost integral to policing, but that there will inevitably be people, both within the police service and outside, who would wish officers to have what many refer to as the 'moral courage and sensitivity' to occasionally bend rules to achieve unquestionably good ends. Put another way, to be 'lawfully audacious' in their approach. It then becomes a question of how far individuals should be prepared to bend the rules. I accept that, as a detective, at whatever level I operated, I was prepared to use every means available to me, within the law, to arrest and deal with offenders. This would often mean being creative and brave on occasions. The issue then becomes one of where the line is drawn. I believe that I always operated within the law. I certainly would never condone the actions of any officers prepared to break the law. The point here is that the reader recognises the inevitability of such dilemmas within policing.

The strength of this argument is that it doesn't resort to the simple formula of moral certainty. Good ends can never justify dirty means. However, it does need to be understood that officers are inevitably confronted with difficult decisions and that the resolution of such problems is itself complex. Nevertheless, the only way that we can ensure that dirty means will not be used too readily or too crudely is to punish those who use them and the agencies that endorse such means. Hence, the advent of the various rules and regulations formally put in place since the 1960s as regards policing.

This whole issue is therefore interesting because I have often spoken to friends, who have never been employed within the police, who see things very simplistically. They expect police officers to use every means possible to achieve a positive outcome and don't appear, on the face of it, to care too much about how this is achieved. However, if the matter affected them or their friends or family in a negative sense, they would no doubt be urging the punishment of police officers who resort to dirty means to achieve some unquestionably good and morally compelling end. Therefore, we need to recognise that we create a 'Dirty Harry' problem for ourselves and for those we urge to effect such punishments. This highlights perfectly the dilemma and dichotomy involved.

In drawing this matter to a conclusion, the danger in 'Dirty Harry' problems is never in their resolution, but in thinking that we may have found a resolution with which we can live. In short, and rather like the question of gratuities received by police officers, the answer is perhaps to openly discuss the issues in a way that both accepts the complex moral world they are involved in, and also helps them recognise the difficult ethical decisions which they will almost certainly be asked to make.

Having now considered the concept of police corruption and misconduct, it is important to focus on how to both deal with it and perhaps prevent it from happening in the first place.

There is now a significant body of evidence from a variety of sources about anti-corruption efforts. In the main, the lessons from this evidence have changed little in the last decade or so. Some of the central lessons, however, now have more supporting evidence, and there is a broader range of material than was available a decade and a half ago. Nevertheless, the central messages seem to remain largely unchanged. Although there are many barriers to successful corruption control, there is evidence that police agencies can be reformed. Also, reform needs to go beyond the immediately identified problem and must look at the political and task environments, as well as the organisation itself. Reform tends not to be durable and continued vigilance and scepticism are vital.

At the heart of much contemporary corruption control, there is the matter of police integrity, and the related issues of how this might be advanced and protected. Police integrity is best thought of as being about officers having the ability to resist temptations to abuse the privileges of their occupation. Integrity has a number of components. It concerns beliefs and not just conduct and is morally charged because it is about right and wrong, combining a belief with an accordance to behave in line with that belief. It involves an inclination to resist, it acknowledges that it is only one source of resistance to misconduct, but it is likely to exert some pressure. It focuses on 'police' rather than 'officer' because it does not necessarily align to the characteristics of individuals but, rather, can also be a characteristic of groups and organisations. By focusing on temptation, it draws attention to the different environments in which the police operate and makes these crucial to understanding conduct. At its core lies the notion of abuse, recognising that corruption is not innocent or defensible and cannot have 'noble causes'.

The promotion and reinforcement of integrity has become a major focus in recent times in police organisations concerned with problems of corruption and misconduct. This has undoubtedly been supported by the much stronger integrity mechanisms now in place. Each force makes continual checks on corrupt activities. Information sharing is transparent in terms of lines of accountability and is also well coordinated.

However, the HMIC, in their 2011 report previously referred to, argued that many forces simply did not have the issue of integrity on their radar and noted that few organisations had successfully resolved the issue of how to promote integrity.

As a means of both measuring and then exploring how police integrity might be enhanced, some American research used scenarios as the basis for examining officers' views, as well as organisational approaches to the issue (Klockars et al 2006 quoted in HMIC *Literature Review - Police Integrity And Corruption.* Professor Tim Newburn London School of Economics & Political Science January 2015). A total of 3,235 officers were asked questions – do they know the rules? How strongly do they support the rules? Do they know what disciplinary threat this agency makes for violation of those rules? Do they think the discipline is fair?

The first question of those taking part should have been, Are the rules clear? The HMIC report referred to suggests that lack of clarity around some of the ethical issues is not uncommon and, logically, this requires clarification before officers can be asked if they understand them. However, this work is considered to have strong validity, as it has now been administered to more than thirty thousand officers in thirty different police agencies and has been correlated with observers' ratings of agency integrity.

Officers were given eleven scenarios. Their answers indicated that they saw some misconduct as being much more serious than others. Four of the eleven cases were not considered very serious at all. These scenarios involved the off-duty operation of a security system business, receipt of free meals, receipt of holiday gifts, and cover-up of a police accident involving driving under the influence of alcohol.

A further four scenarios were considered moderately serious. These involved the excessive use of force on a car thief following a foot pursuit; a supervisor offering an officer time off during holiday in exchange for working on his personal car; acceptance of free drinks in exchange for ignoring a late bar closing; and receipt of a 'kickback'.

Finally, the last three cases were viewed as being profoundly serious - stealing from a found wallet, accepting a financial bribe, and stealing a watch at a crime scene.

It should be noted that all but one of these scenarios concern misconduct motivated by personal gain, the exception being the use of excessive force. It only measures one aspect of integrity, therefore. Nevertheless, the issues it raises are undoubtedly more generally applicable.

The conclusions drawn were that integrity could be fostered in several ways. Firstly, it needs to be treated as something that is central to, and driven by, the organisation's culture. Secondly, rules governing misconduct should be specified and officers trained in their application. Next, the ways in which police managers detect, investigate, and discipline misconduct must show officers how seriously they consider misconduct. Finally, forces should expressly require all officers to report misconduct.

This approach, ie one that seeks to combine clarity about rules and strong enforcement with a variety of approaches to fostering integrity, points to the limitations of punitive approaches to crime control. Clarity around social and legal norms, and an ability to respond quickly and effectively to transgressions, are important elements of any crime control system. However, like public health messages, in many ways the key is prevention.

Consequently, while it is important that forces investigate and punish misconduct, and are seen to do so, it is equally, if not more, important that they engage proactively in the stimulation and maintenance of an organisational culture which has integrity at its core. Following on from the earlier description of integrity, the assumption must be that the processes through which integrity is maintained and enhanced in police organisations are different from those that relate to individuals. To this can be added the observation that strategies should address all types of staff, ie civilian staff and officers at all levels. They should focus on work as well as non-work factors and should involve arrangements for ongoing monitoring of the ethical position of the police service.

Potential solutions linked to this research are detailed as follows:

## Institutional reform

One response to corruption scandals has involved major institutional restructuring or reform. In Belgium, in the aftermath of one scandal, the official inquiry was highly critical of the segmentation of forces, and the rivalry between them, and recommended the creation of a single, national force. In Australia, Commissions of Inquiry, appointed in the aftermath of major scandals in Queensland and New South Wales, adopted much of the then popular new managerialist theory, in proposing sweeping changes to the respective police departments. However, on occasion, structural changes have also been proposed, in particular, focusing on flattening police organisational hierarchies, or to put it another way, a total focus on frontline policing in local area commands under a flatter management structure. Though not proving any direct link, the Queensland and New South Wales forces claimed that such changes contributed to reducing corruption problems in both jurisdictions.

## Investigation and detection

Whatever the seriousness of the misconduct under consideration, police forces need to commit sufficient resources to the investigation and detection of misconduct and corruption. Unfortunately, there is evidence of the failure of forces to thoroughly investigate allegations of, or intelligence concerning, corrupt practices and it is vital that sufficient resources are committed to such activity. In terms of investigating and collecting intelligence, such activity can be described as that which is collected before, during or after the corrupt act. One of the first questions, therefore, is from where can such information/intelligence be drawn?

There are three primary sources, ie members of the public, police officers themselves, and through proactive investigation of police activities. Although corrupt police activity, like much ordinary police activity, is hidden, some intelligence will inevitably come from the public. The bigger question is how prepared and how well organised are police agencies to collect and respond to such intelligence?

Several issues arise here. How can police forces ensure that complaints of corruption are properly and fully recorded? Second, how should police forces treat anonymous reports of corruption and malpractice? The best source of intelligence is that from police officers, ie both honest and corrupt officers, although it is the latter who are of greatest use to investigators. This is very similar to police informants. The most effective sources are those who operate in criminal circles.

Two assumptions about policing and corruption have made agencies shy away from using corrupt officers as a source of proactive intelligence gathering. The first is the continued dominance of the 'few bad apples' idea, something which acts against long term and sustained action against corruption. The second is that police forces are often thought to be overridingly loyal and close-knit. There is a belief in some quarters that the code of silence, the 'Blue Code' previously referred to, is too strong to allow officers to betray their colleagues. That said, much effort in recent times has gone into trying to tackle this so-called blue wall of silence. It is more usual to rely upon officers believed to be untainted by allegations of corruption, and many of the more famous corruption inquiries, the Mollen (New York) and Knapp (Los Angeles, regarding police violence) Commissions in particular, used the support of honest officers in the battle against corruption. In particular, under Commissioner Murphy, the New York Police Department used its field associates programme to recruit large numbers of officers to the cause of reporting on corrupt colleagues.

Integrity testing and covert investigation can both be useful when tackling corruption. Much of the available evidence suggests that proactive investigatory methods are at least as successful as subsequent investigatory work, if not even more effective. Nevertheless, there still appears to be some reluctance among police forces to use such methods. The proactive detection of corruption by internal police units tends, understandably, to be more common in police forces that have, or are concerned about, problems of corrupt practice. Internal affairs or anti-corruption units are established to provide a secure internal investigative capability, as well as offering 'an excuse for being honest'. The most common methods used in such proactive investigation are informants and monitoring of phones and other mobile devices. Additionally, so-called 'corruption patrols' in the US focused primarily on locations known to be frequented by corrupt officers, such as those used for gambling, prostitution, drugs sales and illegal drinking where they were observed for signs of payoffs.

## Integrity testing

Integrity testing is a more controversial tactic in corruption control but is an approach that is increasingly being used. In the UK, the idea of integrity testing has been adapted as one of the proposed responses to the problem of racism following the Macpherson Inquiry. However, such approaches effectively change the central question from 'is the officer corrupt?' to 'is the officer corruptible?' and therefore raise a host of ethical questions, not least in relation to the danger of entrapment.

Integrity tests can be administered both randomly across the workforce and selectively on those where there is some suspicion. Despite the difficulties and the ethical dilemmas raised, integrity testing has become a central theme of corruption control within police forces that have experienced problems. Both NYPD and the Met have had periods where they have invested quite heavily in integrity testing through specialised anti-corruption units. There are suggestions that it has been found to be an effective tool, though as yet there seems little published information that would allow such a claim to be fully assessed.

There are undoubtedly a number of ethical and practical issues raised by proactive and undercover investigation of corruption. These are the potential stimulation of crime that would not otherwise have occurred; the redirection of resources away from crimes known to the police towards possible offences; the potential involvement of police officers in criminal activity; inappropriate behaviour on the part of the state; the protection of criminals, and the non-prosecution of offences committed by those criminals, because of their 'usefulness'; the potential undermining of officers' rights; negative impact, although possibly short-term, on public attitudes toward the police; negative impact on officer morale.

Such ethical concerns, together with the financial costs and the mixed results that random testing has so far produced, have led to considerable restriction in the use of integrity testing within the police service, both in the UK and beyond.

Nonetheless, there are, potentially at least, several areas where integrity testing might reasonably be used, in particular in ensuring procedural compliance. These include how police respond to enquiries and crime reports from the public; how internal affairs officers respond to complaints; how police conduct random breath tests and respond to attempted evasions by off-duty police, for example; how police respond to approaches from ethnic minorities; how police manage domestic disturbances and advise victims of domestic violence.

While intelligence from phone monitoring, direct observation by 'corruption patrol officers' and integrity tests have all proved important in anti-corruption activities, existing evidence suggests that verbal testimony remains the most common source of information. Despite the predominance of standard policing techniques, and the understandable concerns about the use of more proactive or ethically challenging methods of investigation, I think we can conclude that, because of the frequent exposure of police officers to opportunities for corruption, there is a need for more pre-emptive strategies to assist in achieving the ethical standards required. Thus, whilst the evidence for the extended use of random testing is currently quite weak, it is a valid argument to suggest that this is a field in which, at the very least, further experimentation and assessment should undoubtedly take place. The Metropolitan Police have vast experience in this regard and should therefore be called upon to advise other forces.

## Discipline and punishment of corrupt officers

There is little doubt that a robust and fair complaints and discipline system is essential to control misconduct, encourage public confidence in police integrity, and ensure the loyalty and confidence of honest police officers. Given that most intelligence about misconduct derives from complaints, it is vital that the system is easy to access, is appropriately responsive, and itself transparent and accountable.

By 'appropriately responsive', I mean the system should strike a balance between being seen to take allegations seriously, whilst leading to responses that are proportionate to the nature of the alleged misconduct. This balancing act tends to lead to several potential options including:

- An investigative system that is procedurally fair and methodical and is oriented towards finding the truth and applying a just response.
- A proactive system focused on behavioural improvements, primarily through efficient processing of complaints and dispositions, centred on retraining or close supervision.
- In less serious cases, having restorative responses, centred on reconciling conflicts either through mediation between parties or efficient localised forms of communication, explanation and apology.

The standard approach within police forces in recent times has been organised around Professional Standards Departments (PSDs), responsible for investigating complaints. Such units differ from traditional reactive complaints departments in that they proactively cultivate and analyse information on unethical police activity from a range of sources, and mount formal investigations into suspects thereby identified. PSDs are generally divided into an intelligence cell, and one or more operational teams. Information or intelligence enters the intelligence cell, is researched and developed, and then, if it is actionable, is passed to an operational team for investigation.

In terms of complaints and discipline systems, it is my view that the system should be inquisitorial and focused on finding the truth and achieving the best resolution of a matter, before removing officers who commit misconduct or criminal offences.

There needs to be a balance between punitive responses, and remedial and restorative responses.

How effective then are PSDs? I think it is fair to suggest that there remains both an absence of accurate information about, and considerable internal suspicion of, PSDs. Marketing of their work within forces is important, both as a deterrent and to encourage co-operation. There remain issues relating to recruitment of staff, both in terms of attracting the best investigators to such work and reintegrating them when they return to other duties.

Further, I think it is generally the case that more needs to be done to ensure that lessons learned within PSDs are agreed and implemented within forces. Finally, there is a need to ensure that there are sufficient resources for professional standards, not only at a local level but also at regional and national levels, which would complement and increase the capacity of force level units.

## Encourage reporting of misconduct/ whistleblowing

We have already considered the impact of the so-called Blue Code/Wall of Silence. The so-called 'Blue Code' has been identified as an issue by almost every serious commission of inquiry into police corruption. The Wood Commission in New South Wales in 1997 suggested that the code of silence contributed to corruption in at least four main ways. Firstly, for honest and inexperienced officers, it influenced them to accept corruption as part of the job. Second, for managers, it engendered a sense of futility that corruption could be challenged or the police service reformed. Thirdly, for corrupt officers, it was a means by which they could manipulate and control fellow officers. Finally, for internal investigators, it discouraged vigorous inquiry.

Central, therefore, to any successful set of strategies to investigate, detect and prevent police corruption are systems that encourage the reporting of misconduct, or what might these days be referred to as whistleblowing.

Unfortunately, there is little information available about police whistleblowing. An analysis of activity in the aftermath of the Fitzgerald Commission in Queensland found some indication that there was an increased willingness among officers to report misconduct, and this was linked to the greater likelihood of punishment where unreported misconduct was revealed.

Some have argued that compulsory whistleblower legislation is one of those things that is necessary in principle, but its effects on behaviour are unclear or are likely to be weak, due to there being little available material on the issue. One positive way forward might be for police forces to reward the reporting of misconduct and guarantee anonymity. Sadly, despite the development of considerably improved policies toward whistleblowing, it appears that the treatment of such individuals within the public sector still falls far short of what is required if misconduct is to be successfully tackled.

## Monitor propensity for corruption

Corruption is an ever-present risk within police forces and there is clear evidence that a failure to monitor risks is a crucial factor in the potential for the emergence of corruption. Part of the danger lies in the assumption that the propensity for corruption is a current problem and that rigorous recruitment and selection processes would mitigate the problem. Indeed, recruitment and selection processes are a potentially important element in corruption control systems, and it remains important for the police service to be continuously alive to the risks and pressures that might lead towards misconduct. However, this is not, by any means, the silver bullet.

An increasing number of tools are available to the police service, designed to aid the measurement of integrity which, though not perfect, are believed to have proven reliability and are capable of measuring differences and changes in the organisational environments in which they have been employed.

## Enhance recruitment and selection procedures

One regular response by police forces that have experienced significant problems of corruption has involved a substantial reform of a whole range of existing recruitment and selection methods, and implementation of new procedures.

A 1997 Commission on Police Integrity studying corruption in Chicago, the largest US police department outside New York City, recommended higher standards in relation to recruitment and screening, and similar proposals can be found in most reports of major investigations into corruption. Such inquiries have tended to identify many problems with recruitment and selection, such as overwork/ under-staffing of recruitment departments; questionable competence/integrity of staff involved in recruitment; inadequate standards in recruitment or failure to implement normal standards; insufficient background checking/investigation of potential recruits.

Some ideas worthy of consideration should include the automatic exclusion of candidates for disqualifying offences, following criminal history checks. Whilst this seems obvious, there has been a relaxation of what is deemed unacceptable, certainly compared to when I joined. More minor indiscretions are being ignored recently. Next, more rigorous character references, especially from previous employers, should be sought. The use of psychological tests that flag negative character traits is a possibility. The use of drug testing is worth considering. Interviews should probe the ethical awareness and personal principles of applicants, and use follow up investigations of possible adverse indicators. Home visits used to be the norm but again, fell away several years ago. Conducting intelligence checks on associates could be utilised. Perhaps consideration should be given to having a higher recruitment age. However, sadly in my view, the recruitment age has been lowered very recently to just seventeen years of age for potential apprenticeships.

Accepting that there will always be significant resource constraints, I would argue that the bottom line in corruption control is the establishment of a set of clearly defined standards in relation to recruitment, and the operating of these standards with the utmost seriousness. The focus on recruitment, however, is only the first stage of a continuous process that involves training, both of new recruits and established officers and staff.

## Enhance training of officers

Several academics have suggested that it is quite possible to effect behavioural change within forces by imposing strong internal controls which heighten the risk of detection. However, this is far from sufficient and it has been argued that long term change depends more upon embedding high ethical standards than it does on a punitive response to misconduct. Perhaps the answer therefore is it requires a mixture of both.

Reforming training of recruits is perhaps the most common response among police forces attempting to proactively prevent corruption. Historically at least, most police training avoided discussing corruption, and it is a fact that little appears to have changed. On the rare occasions when anti-corruption and ethics did form part of training, it was often done in a manner that was unlikely to resonate with new recruits or make much difference to subsequent behaviour.

In the UK, a series of reports focused very significantly on training. HMIC's (2011) report recommended that, 'Training courses should include appropriate input in relation to integrity and anti-corruption. In particular, given the importance of leadership to securing high standards of integrity... the Strategic Command Course and the High Potential Development Scheme should encompass these issues.'

Nevertheless, and illustrating the difficulties encountered in other organisations, the 2012 follow-up report noted that education on integrity issues within forces was 'patchy' and generally limited to generic training, with, for example, only six forces at that stage providing 'well-structured training in relation to gifts and hospitality'. HMIC similarly found training within police forces to be limited, and often limited to high level statements, rather than detailed policy and procedure. It should therefore be recognised that what research has been conducted suggests that detailed, ongoing in-service training in relation to issues of integrity is vital in corruption control.

## Set official policies and enforce them

Most policing research, both academic and professional, now recognises the central importance of a clear code of ethics to police performance. Hence the development of the Police Code of Ethics. In part, the globalisation of policing has stimulated the development of standards setting, giving rise to a variety of protocols including the European Convention on Human Rights, the Council of Europe's Declaration on the Police, and the Council of Europe's Code of Police Ethics, to mention a few. As with any change within organisations, it is policies that are changed first and then, one hopes, practices change in line with policies.

The area of corruption control is no different. Forces that have struggled with corrupt practices have sought to develop policies that would embed the standards of behaviour expected of staff and outline the general parameters of the organisation's response to the problem.

In addition to formal rules and regulations, there is a need for police forces to construct and adopt an ethical code that makes it clear that there is a wider concern with integrity and ethical behaviour in police work. Equal consideration needs to be given to how officers will be encouraged or persuaded to comply with the standards set out in the code. This is particularly relevant with the still relatively recently developed Police Code of Ethics.

It is sometimes suggested that the adoption of codes will result in unhelpful interference with police discretion and, consequently, a perceived reduction in police effectiveness. This links to the earlier discussion of 'Dirty Harry' problems. This, however, is not the logic of such codes. An elaborate structure of rules is inevitable, given the nature of policing. Such rules do not aim to suppress discretion, but simply to improve its exercise.

At heart, as outlined earlier, lies the issue of ethics, and there are well-established reasons for believing that an emphasis on ethics and integrity is important to tackling corruption in police forces. A Code of Ethics contributes to the image of law enforcement as a profession; helps engender self-respect among individual officers; may contribute to mutual respect among officers and to the development of a positive esprit de corps; provides guidance as to how the law should be enforced.

There is, in this regard, a straightforward link between training, competence and misconduct/ corruption. It means that the better officers are at using legitimate means, the less they will need to have recourse to illegitimate ones.

### Establish robust internal supervision and accountability

Central to all accounts of successful corruption control is the existence and maintenance of robust systems for holding officers and staff, at all levels, to account. All the major investigations into police corruption have highlighted the failures of supervision and management and it has become standard practice to increase or tighten supervision in the aftermath of a corruption scandal. Indeed, one of the implications of rejecting the 'bad apple' theory is that, in order to proliferate, corrupt practices need, at the very least, the implicit support of officers in supervisory and managerial positions.

Therefore, one of the key aspects in any strategy designed to tackle corruption is bringing about a sense of responsibility for integrity among officers and staff. This means ensuring the existence of a form of leadership in which senior officers state explicitly and openly that the ends never justify the means; they are running a department or force with integrity even if this weakens their effectiveness; they will be as open as possible about internal deviance and will co-operate fully with external agencies; they will personally serve as role models for integrity.

The key point of positive leadership is that it sends an unequivocal message to both the department/force and those outside the organisation. To this end, a 2011 review of policing and police leadership, conducted by Peter Neyroud, a former Chief Constable, called for the development of a police professional body with the aim that the service in the future should be driven by public interest and outwardly focused; should evince a firm commitment to ethical leadership, human rights and equality; should be responsible for professional standards for public service in policing.

This led to the development of the College of Policing. However, it must be said that this has received considerable criticism since its inception. In the main, it has not been considered fit for purpose by most police officers, with a lack of hard skills training being available. Additionally, it has been criticised regarding the drive to achieve professionalisation and its role in direct entry to senior levels within the police service.

It has been argued that the key issue for police forces is how to ensure that those in supervisory and managerial positions take responsibility for tackling corruption. One method is to seek to diffuse responsibility for control of misconduct, both vertically and horizontally within the organisation, for example by employing something like the idea of vicarious liability. The intention vertically is that managers should, in some way, be held responsible for the behaviour of their staff. This, the Mollen Commission in New York described as 'reinventing the enforcement of command accountability'. Simultaneously, the aim, horizontally, is also that peers should have an individual and collective responsibility for probity within the ranks. This sounds fine in theory but is very difficult to achieve in practice. Can managers and leaders really be held accountable for the rogue behaviour of some of their staff? Similarly, can peers really be criticised if one of their number goes 'native'?

### Provision of adequate resources for control

In relation to recruitment and selection, it is often the case that the resources committed to any area of policing tend, on occasions, to reflect the seriousness with which forces take such matters. That point can be extended to the whole of corruption control more generally. There is substantial evidence that the cycle of scandal and reform, noted in so many organisations, is a cyclical one. This, at least in part, reflects the rise and fall in the seriousness with which leaders take corruption and, consequently, the extent of the resources they decide to commit to its investigation.

As the Mollen Commission put it in relation to the New York Police Department, 'From the top brass down, there was an often-debilitating fear about police corruption disclosures because it was perceived as an embarrassment to the Department, and likely to engender a loss of public confidence... This attitude infected the entire Department, manifesting itself in different ways throughout the ranks. It encouraged the Department's top managers to allow corruption controls to wither through neglect and denial of resources, and to allow the principle of command accountability to collapse through lack of enforcement.'

### Limit opportunities for corruption

There are areas of policing that, historically, have been found to be more prone to corruption than so-called routine police work. Many of these are predictable and include vice, drugs, undercover policing, informant handling and, to a lesser extent, responsibility for placing contracts, all of which appear to be areas of vulnerability.

Furthermore, there are also procedures that may inadvertently encourage corruption; for example, the setting of unrealistic productivity targets; inadequate means for paying informants/sources; insufficient funds for buying drugs from dealers (test purchasing).

One way of reducing the likelihood of corruption, therefore, is to limit opportunities, either by changing approaches to particular tasks or by introducing new procedures for managing and governing such work.

Specialised units often work particularly well, and subsequently it has been found that, on occasions, their activities have been unduly creative. Therefore, there is a requirement for healthy suspicion and a need to distrust your best performers and high achievers, to some extent. Managers like to see positive results, but they also must continually ask how were such results achieved?

As regards senior officers, while there is a tendency to focus on those on the front line, senior officers have significant power and discretion, often placing them in vulnerable positions. Therefore, it needs to be recognised that no one is immune to contamination, suspicion and scrutiny.

On occasions, laws are difficult or impossible to enforce and where there is limited public support for enforcement, this can provide the conditions that lead to corruption.

## Cultivate a culture intolerant of corruption

One of the best signs of organisational health and corruption resistance is an inbuilt acceptance that the force/department insists on high standards of conduct from its officers and staff. Rather than relying solely on having systems and processes in place to respond when standards are breached, forces should build a strong culture of integrity that pervades the organisation. In addition to having effective corruption control, strategies such as improving investigation and detection procedures; developing a transparent and fair complaints system; establishing robust internal accountability procedures; having clear ethical standards and enforcing these; cultivating a culture that is intolerant of misconduct and refers to the broader question of professionalism and pride in the job, must also be put in place.

Having said this, there is some disagreement over the significance of pride in integrity. A common view is that the more pride police officers have in their department or force, the less likely they will be open to corruption. Fear of detection appears more likely to be more effective in this respect rather than pride in integrity. On the other hand, there are those who believe that deterrence via the threat of prosecution is less likely to have lasting long-term benefits than other more persuasive measures aimed at ensuring compliance.

While cultivating a culture intolerant of corruption is primarily an internal matter, it is also an issue that concerns those outside the police organisation, not least political leaders. That is to say, in just the same way that general lessons for police forces point to the importance of valuing professional standards at all levels, so it is unlikely that police organisations will easily maintain high levels of integrity and conduct if their professionalism is denigrated by political leaders. Those outside the police service, occupying roles in which they have governance responsibilities or oversight for policing, have responsibilities, similar to police leaders, for the establishment and maintenance of a positive image of professional policing. It is right to say that over the years, there have been times when the police service has felt this support has been sadly lacking!

### Establish robust external supervision and accountability

Any discussions on police corruption are effectively unanimous in pointing to the importance of robust external accountability systems as being central to corruption control. Most of what I have referred to so far has focused on internal systems, but there is good reason to believe that any system of corruption control is only as good as the external scrutiny systems that exist.

Over the years, much has been discussed regarding police accountability and it is not relevant to refer to it here. However, suffice it to say that there are several key points that come out of issues involving police misconduct and corruption.

There is considerable evidence that local democratic control over policing is crucial, both to public trust and confidence and to the successful functioning of police forces. However, I am not sure that the advent of Police and Crime Commissioners (PCCs) has achieved this.

Significant civilian involvement in the review of complaints against the police is wanted by both the public and by individual complainants. There is debate and disagreement as to the extent of such citizen oversight, but the general principle is emphasised.

There is a significant correlation between complainant satisfaction and citizen oversight of complaint investigation. Independent Commissions of Inquiry have proved important, both for uncovering corruption and for establishing reformed police departments and forces. Non-police organisations, including media outlets, can play an important role in achieving police reform.

Building on evidence that suggests that police forces with significant corruption problems tend to have inadequate internal control systems, it is vital to have external bodies that oversee the police service's control efforts. Whilst it might be thought that local police oversight bodies, ie PCCs, might reasonably play this role, it can be argued that there is inevitably a variety of tensions that might mitigate the effectiveness of such a relationship.

Similarly, other bodies, such as investigative journalists, specialist commissions of inquiry and even citizen oversight panels, all have shortcomings. In short, current oversight tends to be provided by institutions that are temporary, eg independent commissions. Similarly, the focus of other bodies is either too wide or too narrow, eg PCCs. There are also institutions that at best have the authority to examine only some elements of the agency's control system, eg community oversight panels. The challenge is to design an institution, or set of institutions, that will effectively be able to oversee and control the police service's control system as a whole on a continuous basis. I do not believe that the current IOPC fulfills this role satisfactorily *(see below also)*.

### Detect and investigate corruption not investigated by police forces

Successful corruption control also requires the investigation of corruption that is not, or is not adequately, investigated by the police service. As with the previous point, once again there are likely to be a few individuals or agencies involved in such work. These include lawyers, investigative journalists, individual members of the public and groups representing them. The likelihood is that such activity will be irregular rather than continuous.

Again, the challenge is to design an institution/set of institutions that will tackle this problem more coherently. There are strong arguments currently that the existing IOPC is ineffective and serves the purposes of neither complainants nor serving officers and staff. Therefore, perhaps the solution is a more radical one, creating an agency whose exclusive function would be securing oversight of the police service, in terms of control of corruption and misconduct, continually monitoring its performance, and providing feedback. Perhaps this could be an extension of the existing HMIC (now HMIC&FRS which includes oversight of the Fire Service). The body does not consist entirely of police officers or ex-officers but is a healthy mix of senior individuals from outside the police service as well as those within it.

## Disseminate information about corruption and its control

Finally, and linking back to research evidence on public confidence and trust in policing and its clear links with procedural justice, there are strong arguments for disseminating information about corrupt practices. Although, understandably, there will be those who believe increased publicity around misconduct would undermine public confidence, there are good reasons for thinking that the collection and circulation of robust information about misconduct is an important part of the control effort. Such information provides evidence as to the scale of the problem and indicates that the police service, and indeed others, take the problem seriously. It shows that they will not hide from it and, when the information concerns the investigation, detection and punishment of wrongdoing, provides some basis for deterring misconduct and enhancing integrity. Both the police service and external oversight bodies have responsibilities in this regard.

In the context of so-called 'noble cause' corruption, and to demonstrate how easily a lack of adherence to the disciplinary rules in existence as well as the damage caused through a poor ethical standpoint within an organisation, I am going to use the example of the West Midlands Serious Crime Squad. There are those, even now, who try to undermine the decision of the then Chief Constable, Geoffrey Dear, to disband the squad. However, faced with what he was at the time, it is difficult for any objective individual to argue against it.

The Serious Crime Squad (SCS) was formed in 1974 when West Midlands Police was created by the Local Government Act 1972 which merged Birmingham City Police with parts of several other forces that covered the new West Midlands area.

The Squad's roots go back to 1952, when a Special Crime Squad was formed on an experimental basis. It successfully dealt

*Sir Geoffrey Dear*

with a number of metal thieves, a crime that had grown due to the growth of scrap metal collection from bomb sites in the post-war era. A second Regional Crime Squad was formed with officers from neighbouring counties to deal with crimes outside Birmingham. In 1960, when the squad was known as the Birmingham Crime Squad, it detected over 1,060 crimes a year, and made 579 arrests. However, annual reports emphasise that the seriousness of the crimes, rather than the quantity, was the key factor in performance.

The new squad dealt with the Birmingham pub bombings in 1974, bringing its work to national attention, after the six accused were convicted. It continued to deal with anti-terrorist investigations until 1979, when a separate squad was formed. This meant that the SCS had to reorient its own work primarily towards armed robberies. Also that year, the SCS moved to share offices with other West Midlands police units in the police headquarters building, Lloyd House.

In 1979 and 1980, the SCS investigated a spate of armed robberies known as the Thursday Robberies because, unsurprisingly, they always took place on Thursdays. The gang responsible was known as the Thursday Gang by the police. The SCS and the Robbery Squads worked together in Operation Cat *(see below)* to catch the criminals responsible.

The 1991 independent report into the SCS, commissioned by the Police Complaints Authority with the investigation carried out by West Yorkshire Police, states that 'many Midlands solicitors we have spoken to believe [this operation] gave the green light to some officers... to indulge in serious malpractice'. The arrests included Ronald, Donald and John Brown, whose convictions were later quashed.

In 1980, the SCS arrested John Irvine and Keith Twitchell, known criminals, for armed robbery and the murder of a security guard. Their convictions were also later quashed.

By 1982, the number of arrests made by the SCS had declined to less than two hundred a year, despite the steady increase in reported crime and arrests in the West Midlands. The squad continued to report less than two hundred arrests annually during the 1980s. As a percentage of arrests made by West Midlands Police as a whole, their work was obviously declining. Furthermore, many of the arrests were for crimes categorised as being less serious, with burglary and theft accounting for around half of the arrests made. Explanations, such as criminals becoming more sophisticated and less 'amenable' to making confessions, were suggested. In 1988, the West Midlands Police explained that 'investigations are more protracted, and masks, disguises, false number plates and other means of evading capture are frequently used', techniques which are hardly unusual among hardened criminals committing serious crimes. It was rightly concluded that police management knew that these excuses were thin, and that the squad was under-performing throughout the 1980s.

In 1984, the squad began relying heavily on 'super grass' evidence, which later proved unreliable but did lead to several high-profile arrests. By the mid-1980s, colleagues 'resented the support' of the squad, and thus avoided collaboration, further reducing the squad's ability to pursue serious crime.

The District Auditor strongly criticised the organisation's poor management in 1985 and 1989. The West Midlands police claimed that the SCS was being reorganised in 1988, with changes to recruitment practices, just before it was closed down.

The Police and Criminal Evidence Act of 1984 should have changed many practices at the SCS, for instance by introducing the recording of interviews, and these were noted as having been implemented in the 1986 annual report. Later evidence, however, shows its provisions were widely ignored or evaded.

Throughout the 1980s, there were concerns about the safety of the Birmingham Six convictions in 1975, following the pub bombings, and Chris Mullin MP campaigned to see their convictions reviewed. Similar concerns about the Bridgewater Four, who had been convicted of the murder of 13-year-old paperboy Carl Bridgewater in 1978, after investigation by the sister No 4 Regional Crime Squad, were voiced by the journalist Paul Foot.

Several cases had been overturned in the 1980s and several members of the squad were seen as unreliable witnesses. However, concerns were now given new credence, due to what was then a new forensic technique using a machine known as an ESDA, or Electrostatic Detection Apparatus. The technique allowed forensic experts to trace impressions made on sheets of paper underneath the original, often showing when words or lines had been added to original statements. The first case to use this evidence was that of Paul Dandy, in 1987.

In January 1989 Clare Short, MP for Birmingham Ladywood, raised in Parliament the problems that Birmingham solicitors had encountered when trying to raise complaints about their clients' cases in relation to the squad. She detailed the apparently widespread practice the squad employed of doctoring statements by adding additional incriminating pages, which was leading to certain convictions being challenged.

Nevertheless, the systemic issues at the West Midlands SCS were not being addressed, such as the apparent culture of taking shortcuts and abusing procedure in order to perform well enough for individuals to qualify for promotion.

In August 1989, the squad was disbanded by Chief Constable Geoffrey Dear and a few of its senior officers were put on desk duties. In the same month, an investigation by West Yorkshire Police, led by Assistant Chief Constable Donald Shaw, was asked to examine allegations of misconduct involving the squad. However, its remit was limited to complaints made after the start of 1986 'when complaints about the squad started to emerge'. The question of whether the convictions in the Birmingham pub bombings case were safe was raised at the time but was considered out of scope and unnecessary by the government. A number of the former SCS officers who had been placed on desk duties were returned to investigatory roles in 1990, after Dear left for another post and was replaced by Ronald Hadfield.

The official PCA (Police Complaints Authority) report, published in 1994, concluded there had been 'physical abuse of prisoners, fabrication of admissions, planting of evidence and mishandling of informants'. Yet just seven officers faced disciplinary action, for twenty-eight disciplinary complaints. One officer faced a complaint about tampering with a statement, while the other six were suspected of irregularities relating to payments to informers. A further ten officers would have faced twenty complaints but had left or retired. Another 102 officers were given informal advice about their failures to adhere to police procedures. The disciplinary procedures were conducted as an internal matter. However, the report recommended that no officers should face criminal charges.

The Director of Public Prosecutions, Barbara Mills, agreed that there was insufficient evidence to prosecute any officer from the squad, a decision for which she was widely criticised. Although no officers were prosecuted for their roles in corrupt investigations, former West Midlands Serious Crime Squad detective Laurence Henry Shaw was later convicted of attempted robbery in Solihull in 2001 and, in 2010, for armed robbery in Lostwithiel, Cornwall.

What is significant in terms of operational culture was the fact that the SCS suffered from several issues, ranging from poor recruitment and management practices to well-documented and repeated techniques of falsification. Poor management led to poor performance, which in turn exacerbated the pressure to take shortcuts. There was arguably far too much freedom which allowed for poor practice or worse to take place.

The SCS had an elite ethos, which may have induced a certain amount of arrogance when dealing with other investigators. Recruitment was usually through choice rather than open recruitment. The SCS was an all-male and, it was believed, a wholly white unit. Officers tended to serve for long periods rather than move regularly. Officers were allowed to work exceptionally long overtime hours. There are also recorded incidents of bullying of officers who reported malpractice. These factors may have together reinforced an insular culture.

One specific example is cited here. The general West Midlands interview manual was criticised as being misleading, advising officers to assume a suspect was guilty, in a range of situations where this may not have been true. The manual appeared to be a compendium of techniques and experience from officers, rather than being based on independent psychological research and evidence. Reactions by detainees in interview can be made under stress and therefore need to be treated with caution. However, the manual instead offered interpretations of various reactions as likely signs of guilt, often including contradictory interpretations of similar reactions, without codifying or recognising this. For instance, insisting on innocence and complaining about treatment was signalled, in different parts of the manual, as indicating both innocence and guilt. *The Guardian* concluded that West Midlands Police should 'adopt the approach of the Mersey scheme, with its emphasis on teaching the police to listen and frame questions. Research shows the biggest mistake in interrogation is the failure to listen to what is said.'

There was a lax approach to the pairing of officers for interview. Officers who are less familiar with each other should be put together to reduce risks of poor or illegal practice. A number of regular pairings of interviewing officers seems to have led to collaboration in falsifying evidence.

It was West Midlands police policy to transfer most documents to microfiche after two years and destroy the originals. Often, the microfiche copies were unreadable. The practice also made it impossible to ascertain, through ESDA scanning and analysis, if statements had been interfered with.

Low level paperwork tasks were supervised by upper management, which was in general too involved in practical work including investigations, distracting from leadership, policy setting and supervision. Management focused on paper-based processes and individuals were given little management training. Junior officers appeared to have a practical veto on new recruits.

Management practice was sufficiently poor for misleading statements to be made by the squad to external authorities. For instance, it told the Court of Appeal that officers had been disciplined after interference with witness statements, but that the changes did not include 'incriminating admissions', which was wholly untrue. As a result, appeals of two men named Horobin and Wilcox were rejected in 1988.

The SCS often relied on confessions to the exclusion of other kinds of evidence, even though they are inherently unreliable. Sometimes, this can simply be due to the presence of authority and the expectation to confess. It can be due to stress factors in interviews. Given a certain level of stress, some interviewees will confess simply to bring the experience to a stop. A third group may come to believe in their guilt over time. Thus false confessions are not the product of coercive techniques alone, but these factors can make confessions unsound.

The Civil Liberties Trust funded Birmingham University legal academic Tim Kaye to lead an independent inquiry, backed by an advisory panel including Clare Short and the Bishop of Birmingham, Mark Santer. It reported in 1991, three years before the official inquiry undertaken by West Yorkshire Police, and presented evidence of systemic malpractice and patterns of fabrication of evidence and other procedural abuses by specific officers.

The inquiry noted five cases where a statement with a confession was presented to other suspects, and self-incriminating reactions were noted, although not usually signed by the suspects. This evidence was then used in their convictions. For instance, a defendant, Michael Foran *(see below)*, was noted as saying, 'What can I say? It's all there, isn't it?' Another, Derek Boswell *(see below)*, was recorded as saying, 'That fucking bastard, I'll kill him... we all agreed to make our own statements if caught and I can't make one against my own will, can I?'

Several confessions were said by police officers to have taken place in a squad car immediately after arrest. Sometimes, the suspects were taken to police stations some distance away from the arrest in contravention of PACE regulations. Squad car interviews represent an opportunity to interview suspects without a solicitor and make it relatively easy for officers to claim that incriminating statements were made, including falsification of signed notes.

To make it hard for interviewees to be found by lawyers or relatives, police used haphazard interview locations, often to the annoyance of other police, especially as they would be implicitly tolerating the denial of suspects' rights to a solicitor. Arrests regularly took place very early in the morning, which is often standard police practice to ensure suspects are easily located but would have made them disoriented at interview. Irregular, long and early hours would also have affected police performance.

Forensic ESDA evidence showed that signed confessions from Paul Dandy's case *(see below)* had been tampered with. However, the original statements were generally destroyed, as noted above, making it impossible to make this analysis in most cases. Instead, courts later worked on the assumption that certain officers may have tampered with signed confessions based on previous behaviour, making a conviction unsafe if it relied on this evidence.

Many confessions were recorded but not admitted to by defendants. The confessional statements were generally short and lacked detail, even during long interviews. Kaye noted that such confessions would be unusual as most of the suspects were criminals with several convictions, so were likely to be familiar with police procedure and the effect of such convictions, if they were insisting on their innocence.

Kaye added that the language of the statements was generally remarkably similar, lacking differentiation in phraseology and colloquialisms, whether from Birmingham or the Black Country. He recorded that many of them were variants on 'That's a bit heavy', 'You're spot on', 'That bastard's really put me in it' and 'You're putting a good case against me'. Additionally, they did not reflect the diverse backgrounds of the suspects, who may have been Asian, African Caribbean or from different regions of Britain or Ireland. Only in the case of African Caribbeans did he note any difference, where suspects would use the word 'man', despite using the same language patterns in every other respect.

Other evidence for interference comes from the length of the statements. Where their content is claimed to have been added to, these frequently show implausibly fast note taking. Kaye calculates the transcription rate as being around thirty words a minute, rather than a more typical twenty to twenty-three a minute. In John O'Brien's case *(see below)*, an officer named DC Shaw was asked in court to read back his notes from an interview that was marked as having taken fifteen minutes. He took twenty minutes to read them back. The case was dropped.

Kaye's analysis of 1980s case evidence found that no confession evidence was produced when a solicitor was present. He also found that access to solicitors was delayed in every case, except those where no request was made. In other words, if no solicitor was requested, then there could be no delay. It appears therefore that the standard practice was to interview suspects with the aim of gaining a confession, prior to allowing them a solicitor. Nevertheless, this did not stop the confession evidence being used in successful trials.

In some cases, suspects were forced to sign custody records stating that they had not requested a solicitor. In one case, involving a man named George Lewis, the custody sheet had a line marking the paper where his hand has clearly been knocked to prevent him striking out the statement saying he had agreed not to have a solicitor present. In another case involving a man named Charles Campbell, his solicitor, a Mr Shipley, obtained the agreement of the police that no interview was to take place without his presence, but Campbell's confession was still apparently obtained in an interview within fifteen minutes of his departure.

Super grass evidence was used to corroborate evidence from alleged confessions. It did not appear alongside other evidence, according to Kaye, so cases relied on a combination of confession and super grass evidence. On reflection, the court probably should not have allowed it, due to such evidence being unsafe.

Operation Cat, already mentioned, relied heavily on evidence from a super grass named Keith Morgan. Morgan had admitted twenty offences and was sentenced to five years' imprisonment in return for the evidence he presented. He was not a reliable witness, however. He had also alleged that a Merseyside police officer helped him plan some robberies and demanded payment. These allegations were dismissed after an investigation. The fact involving this allegation and its unreliability was not available to the defence team.

Super grass Albert McCabe implicated over a hundred suspects from 1986, many of whom were prosecuted, but whose cases later collapsed. He was prosecuted himself for a small number of offences, admitting nearly seventy, and sentenced to six years in jail, the light sentence being part of the deal for giving evidence against others. He later wrote to the solicitors of those he had implicated to explain that his evidence was provided under duress. Once convicted, he refused to make any further statements to the police.

Allegations were made in the early 1980s that SCS officers placed plastic bags over the heads of suspects, and covered their mouths, to partially suffocate them and extract a confession. Kaye noted that no allegations occurred after 1983. In the case of Keith Twitchell in 1980 *(see below)*, he underwent a polygraph test and a 'truth drug' test to try to establish that this had happened, but the evidence was deemed inadmissible by the court at the time.

In 1982 to 1983, some of the accused in the Operation Cat convictions made the same allegation. In Derek Treadaway's case, a Home Office pathologist gave evidence that abrasions around his mouth and bruising on his shoulders and chest were consistent with his account of being held down on a chair and 'plastic bagged' with his mouth covered.

Allegations of violence declined, with many fewer such claims being made after 1986, according to Kaye. Explanations for the decline in violence may include that it proved counter-productive, as evidence of physical abuse could be recorded and presented in court, and that psychological pressure in obtaining confessions could be just as effective.

However, there were many serious allegations of violence towards suspects in the SCS's earlier history, the best known of which are those of the Birmingham Six. Derek Boswell made well-documented allegations in 1983, after he refused to make a statement. He claimed that an unknown officer entered his cell, beat him up and told him to make a statement. He was later visited by a doctor who recorded that he had blood stains on his T-shirt and trousers, blood clots in his nostrils and minor facial injuries, consistent with his account of being hit in the face. The officer was never identified, although Boswell gave a description of him at the time. One SCS officer was convicted in 1983 of beating up suspects on the evidence of a police cadet, who was subsequently ostracised and resigned.

As violence declined, complaints of threats grew, according to Kaye. Another defendant, Paul Fitzsimmons, alleged that he was threatened while in prison with re-arrest on release, unless he supported the police's account of solicitors asking for bribes in the case of Ronnie Bolden. An officer named DS McManus is alleged to have asked Fitzsimmons to claim that Bolden's solicitors had offered him a bribe to give evidence to help Bolden.

Hassan Khan claimed that he was told, during his journey back following his arrest in North Wales, that he would be beaten up and treated in the same way as the Birmingham Six, and that he was going to meet the person who dealt with them.

Eileen McCabe, the sister of super grass Albert McCabe, said she was told to sign a confession. Her children were brought to the police station, despite prior agreement that they were to stay with their grandmother, which made her extremely concerned about how they were being treated. She signed the confession, but it later came to light that she had difficulty reading so was unlikely to have understood its contents.

George Lewis alleged that he was threatened with a syringe, with police saying they would give him injections, which he feared, if he did not sign. A witness in the case of the alleged murder of an officer named PC Salt also claimed she was intimidated and shouted at while being told to implicate the others involved, while the main suspects were threatened with the murder charges if they did not confess to robbing him.

In some cases, the SCS was accused of fabricating forensic evidence. Ronnie Bolden alleged that police rubbed his shoes and socks on a getaway car's carpet. In the case of Robert Burston, police were said to have taken bin liners with his fingerprints and placed them in a post office van. Keith Twitchell claimed his hairs were planted as evidence, although this was not used in court.

During the PCA inquiry previously referred to which began in 1991, seven police notebooks were found to be missing, despite it being a requirement for these to be kept secure for seven years. Six arrest files out of 658 for the period 1986 to August 1989 were also missing. Kaye concluded that files going missing 'was not uncommon' at the SCS. In the case of an individual named Gall, this included witness statements from the assault victim which described the assailant as hugely different in appearance from Gall. This evidence did re-appear, late in the court case, but Gall was still convicted. It is not clear as to whether his conviction was the subject of an appeal.

Michael Brommell, convicted of shotgun offences, complained about a fabricated confession. However, the interview notes had gone missing, making it impossible to identify the officers who had taken them. Nevertheless, two officers had viewed the file containing these notes, the day before they went missing. The officers were suspended when the SCS was disbanded, but reinstated after it was found that there was no evidence they had removed the notes.

Some cases relied on timing evidence which may have been altered. For instance, Michael Foran was said to have been arrested at 3.05pm, just after an accomplice had arranged to meet him at Hurst Street car park. However, Foran was logged as being in a cell by 3.12pm, a mere seven minutes later. Foran claimed to have been arrested at 2.05pm. An entry on his arrest sheet was crossed out. However, the original document was destroyed so could not be examined.

Timing evidence was also important in the Birmingham Six case, where a forensic scientist, Dr Frank Skuse, stated he examined the suspects and found them in good health at a time that was later than the time at which they claimed they had been beaten up. However, he had not taken notes, and a local chemist had been contacted by him at a time compatible with the defence's account.

The following represent cases of note, some of which have been mentioned above.

### Paul Dandy

Dandy's case was the first where ESDA evidence showed that tampering with statements had taken place at the SCS, and opened up the possibility of re-examining the cases of others, who had complained but not been believed.

In 1987, Dandy spent eighteen months in prison, on remand awaiting trial for armed robbery. His defence presented forensic evidence from an ESDA examination which showed his statement may have been tampered with, with a one-line confession from Dandy added. The case collapsed. In 1993, Dandy was awarded £70,000 compensation for his time in detention on remand. The police officers concerned were disciplined internally, and a report given to the CPS to consider further action.

### Peter Gibbs, Mark Samuels and Tony Francis

Gibbs, Samuels and Francis were accused of being involved in the death of PC Tony Salt. Salt had been on duty with PC Mark Berry on 16 April 1989 in Small Heath, supposedly watching an illegal nightclub from a flat. According to Chris Mullin MP, recounting the events in Parliament, Salt most likely died after a bout of heavy drinking while on duty, which led to his collapse. Mullin states Berry made four statements, which gradually increased the number and involvement of one to three black men in the incident, one of whom was said to have dreadlocks.

At a press conference the day after the death, Assistant Chief Constable Meffen asserted that 'PC Salt had broken cover to check a suspect car and was set upon by a person or persons with martial arts skills, dragged into the alley and beaten to death,' although these details did not appear in any of the statements made by PC Mark Berry.

Gibbs, Samuels and Francis were arrested and interviewed. None had dreadlocks. Mullin stated: 'Mr Gibbs... describes how, once he had agreed to admit the thefts, he was carefully rehearsed in what he was to say, once the recorder was switched on: "They were saying you can either do it peacefully or we can do it rough. I've been beaten up before in police stations and it's not very nice. I wasn't prepared to go through all that again." ' Eventually, he agreed to admit to stealing PC Salt's wallet and a martial arts weapon called a kubaton that Salt was thought to be carrying.

According to Mullin, Samuels confessed to theft after being threatened with being charged with murder. Francis was told that his family would be set up on drugs charges if he did not confess to theft, while another witness was told to say she had witnessed Francis hitting Salt. After securing their confessions for theft, all three men were charged with murder.

However, the case against the three quickly unravelled. A taxi driver had witnessed Salt and Berry's drinking bout. Salt's wife said that she had found the kubaton that two of the suspects had confessed to stealing and stated that Salt had taken no more than £5 with him that night, rather than the £30 said to have been stolen. The pathologist showed that, although Salt had suffered a blow to the neck, he could not have then walked 120' from the party to the place where he died. According to Mullin, the pathologist stated that 'the most likely explanation for his death was that, in his drunken state, Mr Salt had fallen and hit his head on the bucket of a JCB digger parked nearby'.

The charges were dropped, although only a year after the original events, despite the strength of evidence that the three accused were innocent.

The Police Federation included Salt on the Roll of Honour of officers who fell in the line of duty. His name was also included on the memorial in the West Midlands Police headquarters on Colmore Row, as well as the National Police Memorial in London where it remains, despite the subsequent findings.

Around forty convictions failed in the 1980s, and a further sixty convictions have since been overturned. This is a summary of those cases where there has been news reporting or the judgment has been published.

### Birmingham Six

The Birmingham Six, Hugh Callaghan, Patrick Joseph Hill, Gerard Hunter, Richard McIlkenny, William Power and John Walker, were each sentenced to life imprisonment in 1975, following their false convictions for the 1974 Birmingham pub bombings. Their convictions were declared unjust and unsatisfactory and were quashed by the Court of Appeal on 14 March 1991. The six men were later awarded compensation ranging from £840,000 to £1.2 million.

### Derek Treadaway, Michael Dunne, Ronald, Donald and John Brown

Derek Treadaway, Michael Dunne, Ronald, Donald and John Brown were arrested in Operation Cat and accused of being members of the so-called Thursday Gang, named after a series of post office robberies which were committed on Thursdays.

*Birmingham Six*

Treadaway was convicted in 1983 of three post office robberies committed in 1979 in Erdington and elsewhere. His conviction was overturned in 1996. He was a victim of 'bagging', that is, use of a plastic bag to suffocate interviewees to extract a confession. He alleged at a civil trial for damages that his confession was the false product of police impropriety in handcuffing him, placing plastic bags over his head to suffocate him, and forcing him to sign the written confession which had already been prepared for signature by police officers. There was evidence in the criminal trial that he had sustained petechial haemorrhages on his breastbone, about which a doctor gave evidence for the defence. He also complained during the criminal trial that he had been deliberately denied access to a solicitor.

Other evidence that was relied on at trial came from super grass witnesses, whose close involvement with corrupt officers made their testimony dubious. Several of the officers involved failed to turn up to the appeal hearings.

Ronald, Donald and John Brown, also convicted for the robberies, had their convictions overturned later, in two separate appeals.

## George Glen Lewis

Lewis was arrested in January 1987 and subsequently convicted of two armed robberies and a burglary. His case was examined by the Yorkshire Police during their investigation.

He told the Court of Appeal that he was head butted, punched and threatened with a syringe as he was questioned. He was forced to sign a confession and was also racially abused. ESDA evidence of the impressions left by his signatures showed it was likely he had signed blank sheets of paper. These were then used to write a statement in reverse order to that in which it was signed. In other words, the imprints of the signatures showed that, when they were made, the pages were in a different order to how they appeared after the statement was filled in.

His conviction relied on the evidence of Detective Constable John Perkins and Detective Constable Peter Reynolds, who stated that Lewis confessed while they were driving to the police station after his arrest. Perkins allegedly refused to allow Lewis a solicitor, threatened him, punched him and demanded that he sign blank interview sheets.

Lewis served five and half years in prison and was awarded £200,000 in compensation when his conviction was quashed.

## Keith Twitchell, John Lyon McCloy and Patrick Irvine

Twitchell, McCloy and Irvine were arrested and convicted of involvement in a robbery in 1980. Twitchell claimed at trial that police had handcuffed him to the back legs of the chair he was sitting on, placed a plastic bag over his head and pressed the material to his nose and mouth. His solicitor, Mr Solley, stated at the trial that the 'bag was removed from his head. The procedure was repeated a number of times, until finally his resolve was totally dissolved and he agreed to sign the statement put in front of him'. A policeman was alleged to have threatened that 'the bastard signs or he goes feet first'. Twitchell complained about being 'bagged' at the time. He was denied access to a solicitor until he had signed a statement. All three had their convictions quashed.

### Tarlochan Singh Gill and three others

Gill was convicted in 1984 of the murder of Wati Suri during a burglary. She was beaten and strangled. Three other men allegedly involved were found guilty but their convictions were quashed in 1985. Gill's conviction, however, was upheld, based on a confession he was said to have made. He had spent ten years in jail by the time his conviction was finally quashed on the basis that his confession was extracted by Detective Sergeant James, whose evidence had been found to be unreliable in three other cases. As Gill's conviction relied on that evidence, it was also found to be unsafe and was quashed.

### John Joseph Cumminskey and Roy Meads

Cumminskey and Meads were convicted of armed robbery of £185,000 from a postal van. They separately had their convictions quashed. Roy Meads' conviction was quashed in January 1996.

Cumminskey was jailed in 1985 and served eight years of a fifteen-year sentence. He asked for leave to appeal in 1987 but was refused. His second request in 1999 followed the review of other cases by the Criminal Cases Review Commission. His appeal was granted in 2003, following a further review of his case.

### David Murphy and Patrick O'Toole

Murphy and O'Toole were convicted in 1978 of armed robbery at a British Leyland plant at Ward End. Murphy received eight years and O'Toole seven.

On appeal, the court noted that Murphy said he was abused and intimidated by the police and had made no confessions. O'Toole said that, when he refused to make a statement admitting his part in the robbery, he was beaten up by police officers, especially by a DS Matthews.

Their convictions were quashed in 2006, as the conviction, in the view of the court, 'critically depended on the evidence of police officers, notably Hornby and Matthews, whose characters have subsequently been gravely tainted, especially that of Hornby'.

## Martin Foran

Foran was convicted of four counts of robbery in 1978. He was arrested and convicted again in 1984 for a pub robbery. Both convictions were quashed, in 2013 and 2014. In 2013, reviewing the conviction for the 1984 offence, the courts found that police had ignored evidence that the 'Martin' sought was a 'kid' and that tampering with statements had been widespread in the squad at the time and in particular, evidence handled by (the now) DI Matthews was unreliable. The defence had also been denied access to evidence that could have helped them.

The No 4 Regional Crime Squad, which led the investigation, was a sister squad to the SCS, operating over a wider area. Many of its officers were recruited to the SCS, including several who were later involved in misconduct.

## Bridgewater Four

The Bridgewater Four were Patrick Molloy, James Robinson and cousins Michael and Vincent Hickey. On 21 February 1997, the last in a number of appeals saw their convictions overturned, after the Court of Appeal ruled that the trial had been unfair, as certain areas of evidence had been fabricated by police in order to persuade the by then deceased Molloy to confess. However, the Appeal Judges noted that, in the light of Vincent Hickey's confessions to being present at the farm where Bridgewater was shot dead, 'we consider that there remains evidence on which a reasonable jury, properly directed, could convict'.

The officers involved were later employed at the West Midlands Serious Crime Squad.

There is little doubt, when considering the issues involving the West Midlands Serious Crime Squad, that many of their practices amounted to so-called 'noble cause' corruption. Because most of the individuals arrested and convicted had criminal records, assumptions were made about their guilt and they were 'fitted up' as a result. It appears that the senior managers were party to what was happening and indeed, were often directly involved, or at least complicit. It is cases such as these that totally undermine the police service and those honest hard-working officers operating within it. Geoffrey Dear was totally correct, in my opinion, to disband the Squad. It was the only way that public confidence could ever be restored.

The cause for greatest concern is that so few officers ultimately faced misconduct proceedings. Indeed, there is no doubt that a number should have been subjected to criminal proceedings. We are sadly left to assume that there was insufficient evidence available to substantiate criminal charges. In cases such as these, it is difficult to mount successful prosecutions because the vast majority of the officers involved are all implicated to a greater or lesser extent. Cases therefore would rely on the word of convicted criminals who would clearly not make good witnesses, for obvious reasons!

# CHAPTER 6

## Undercover policing and police informants

In the context of a potential lack of integrity, the use of informants, now known as CHIS (Covert Human Intelligence Sources), is possibly the highest risk area in today's police service. Indeed, the use of informants by the police is probably viewed by the average member of the public as somewhat distasteful. The image portrayed in fictional representation of detectives meeting with their 'snouts', who more often than not are criminals themselves, and giving them a 'bung' (money) for information against other criminals, appears seedy, to say the least!

However, since the publication of the report *Helping with Enquiries: Tackling Crime Effectively* (1993) by the Audit Commission, there has been an increasing reliance on intelligence-led policing, which necessarily includes the use of informants. There is nothing new about using informants but it has been suggested at various times, even by those inside the organisation, that their use causes so much controversy and difficulty, for both the police service and individual informant handlers, with limited benefit, that it should be stopped altogether. It is, however, a fact that many people in law enforcement still believe informants are valuable and necessary.

If informants are properly targeted and controlled, they can be an invaluable and relatively inexpensive police resource. Some other law enforcement agencies believe the main reason their staff are less susceptible to corruption is because police officers are exposed to criminals far more frequently and in a less controlled environment. It is vital, therefore, to have good controlling mechanisms in informant handling. Historically, it is correct to say that often effective systems for ensuring informants were used with integrity either did not exist at all or were ignored.

There has been an enormous amount of hard work by many officers over the years to ensure a steady flow of high-grade intelligence. The police service should fully support and value those who recruit and handle informants, often in difficult and time-consuming circumstances. Whilst every effort should be made to ensure integrity, a siege mentality should not be allowed to develop among the overwhelming number of honest officers working in this difficult field. They are not the enemy, but any corrupt officers and treacherous informants are.

The guidance and rules governing the handling of informants in more recent times have been intended to support officers who handle or control informants with integrity, and not to hinder them. It is a fact that many major criminals have recruited themselves as informants over the years, giving low grade information, often about minor crime, in exchange for perhaps a letter of mitigation to a judge, or bail when they would otherwise be kept in custody. Such letters are known as 'texts'. Money is rarely an incentive for these people. They simply see being a registered informant as an insurance policy for when they are arrested or, in some cases, a means of removing their competition, particularly perhaps in the case of drug dealers.

As a result, there is an acknowledged risk that inexperienced handlers of such major criminals could find themselves out of their depth and being led by the informant, rather than doing the leading. The question of risk assessment is therefore now always considered, in that, if the police, by using such informants, are facilitating them in committing more serious crime than they are helping to detect, their use clearly lacks integrity and is counterproductive. In order to go some way to controlling 'hidden' rewards, such as the cancellation of a parking ticket or the granting of bail when custody would normally be sought, the same methods of authorisation and auditing as would be applied to a cash payment are, nowadays, applied to every benefit received by an informant.

It has always been something of a grey area as regards when a person giving information comes within the definition of being an informant. Some people who give information to the police do not want to be registered as an informant and some may not seem worthy of registration. Should an officer, for example, register an elderly lady who, on a regular basis, passes details of car registration numbers leaving a suspect's address opposite her own?

As a result, forces now run 'Confidential Source' systems which allow for the recording of specified people without registering them as informants. These practices should always be carefully controlled to ensure they are not used as a backdoor method of avoiding stringent control systems.

Historically, it is sadly a fact that the quality of supervision given to informant handlers was, in the main, seriously inadequate. For the benefit of non-police readers, an informant controller is the supervisor or manager of the officer who is the informant handler. There were times when it was generally believed that informant controllers were too remote from their handlers and were untrained and generally trying to control too many informants. It is also the case that informants were rarely, if indeed ever, even seen by the controller, making it impossible for their identity to be verified, or for there to have been a first-hand assessment of their value or the risk they may pose.

In the past, informant handling and controlling was most often not the sole task of such officers and with the advent of the wider use of properly registered informants, it was clearly unrealistic to expect a controller to manage more than twenty to twenty-five informants. Around the end of the 1990s, detective inspectors were often expected to control a hundred or more informants, of whom perhaps only twenty were active and passing good quality information. Following an HMIC report in 1999, forces were asked to question the value of having large numbers of unproductive informants, which prevented the adequate supervision of officers handling those of higher quality. With the subsequent development of specialist CHIS handling teams, this resulted in dispensing with the services of those informants who did not produce a regular, valuable product. One of the unfortunate by-products of the intelligence-led approach is that, in some areas, officers were being urged to recruit informants with little regard for quality, to try to reach arbitrarily set performance targets. There were indeed reported examples, in some forces, of officers being told that, to gain recruitment to and remain in the CID, they would need to have a pre-determined number of registered informants. Inevitably, this produced a glut of low-grade informants, the supervision of whom deflected the controller's efforts away from those who required most attention. To ensure a valuable product was being obtained, and to dispense with those where it was not, forces were required to assess the activity of their informants at far more regular intervals.

Nowadays, all matters relating the conduct and control of sources and their management are dealt with through Home Office-approved IT systems, such as the police informant management system (PIMS). I believe this system has been recently updated or replaced. This is also used to produce management data and assist with the monitoring of informant handling activity, thus enabling managers to maintain a strategic view of informant use and to improve the general integrity of the whole procedure. This is without doubt one of the absolute best developments in recent years in efforts to improve the integrity of informant handling.

Over the years, considerable issues arose regarding reward payments made to informants. Gone are the days when officers gave informants money out of their own pockets and then made claims to compensate. There were also issues with timeliness of payments, and cases found by HMIC where officers could wait two months while the paperwork was going through a laborious finance system. Where informants demand payment, they usually expect it quickly and it is unprofessional and an unacceptable burden on handlers for them to have to explain to informants the vagaries of their force accounting systems.

In recent times, the system has developed a far more professional approach. Now, the current rewards system even lays down the amount of payments for certain categories of information. With the advent of online banking, there are alternative methods of rewarding informants other than by cash payments. This again reduces the potential for any corrupt activity and does not allow for the possibility of misappropriation. Verification of the fact the informant received the reward is essential to discount any suggestion of impropriety. As a result, payments to informants are witnessed by the controller.

Again, historically there was a major concern within the service that there was either insufficient or no training for informant handlers and controllers. This has led to the professionalisation of this field, to the extent where national standards prevail, overseen by the College of Policing. Courses are accredited, based on the new national standards for covert policing, drawn up by the National Police Chiefs Council. New Manuals of Guidance, together with their accompanying Codes of Practice, have been in existence for some time and they will hopefully go some way to reassuring the public that the police are doing all they can to ensure integrity in their very necessary covert operations. One facet of the new guidance is that all officers who handle informants must be properly trained and accredited.

Again, one of the more recent developments has seen an officer of the rank of detective superintendent appointed to oversee and manage CABs or Central Authorities Bureaux, in order to achieve independent oversight. These individuals are therefore not involved directly in any investigations and can, as a result, provide a more consistent application and independent scrutiny of the whole process. They will randomly inspect the integrity of such cases and the use of the informant. The essential aspect is that they have unfettered access to all records relating to a force's informants and, if necessary, the informants themselves. In all forces now, active informants and their handlers are subject to intense scrutiny, including examination of contact reports, mobile phones and payments, to determine any significant or untoward trends. However, it is done openly and officers are aware of the checks. There is now in existence an acknowledged need to be open and vigorous in terms of auditing the handling and control of informants.

As I have previously mentioned, dedicated Source Units are now in place to handle all informants. This has helped considerably to remove the potential for corrupt activity between informant and handling officer and reduces the likelihood of what is known as 'status drift'. This is where an officer recruits an informant or source and then acts directly on the information or intelligence provided. The current system reduces the risks to the informants themselves as well as the recruiting officer, as an automatic 'sterile corridor' is now produced, and the source is handed over to an officer in the Source Unit. Therefore, there is no potential for information to be linked back to that recruiting officer and therefore reduces the likelihood of compromising the source.

This level of professionalisation of informant management is therefore enhanced through the recruitment of hand-picked detectives of proven ability and integrity. This development also challenges the long-held myth that an informant 'will only deal with me'. Such statements are patently untrue, and if, in individual instances, it is the case, the use of that informant is unacceptable and he/she should be de-registered.

A culture should exist whereby informants are truly considered to be the property of the organisation, rather than the individual. Many of the problems in the past have been because an unhealthy, close relationship built up between informant and handler. This has been likened to the Stockholm Syndrome, when, as sometimes happens, a bonding occurs between hostages and hijackers. It was not unusual in the past to find examples where officers had run informants for many years, with the two people moving up through the police and criminal hierarchy simultaneously. I will shortly refer to a case where exactly this happened, with dire consequences. Clearly, over such periods of time, there is the risk the boundary with impropriety can be blurred, the police officer can become very protective of his or her source and in some cases, this can result in the handler being used by the informant and, potentially, the informant even being protected from arrest. In some cases, therefore, a potential solution is to develop a strict tenure policy, whereby a source can only be handled by the same individual for a maximum of two years. In these circumstances, the selection of the new handler should be done by managers and not by the informant or outgoing handler.

Nowadays therefore, informants should be regarded as a corporate asset with controllers responsible only for the number of informants they can properly supervise, and handlers changed at set intervals.

Even allowing for the recent positive developments in the management of informants, it is still inevitably a controversial area of policing. Just a few years ago, an informant in the Newcastle child sex case, a convicted child rapist, claimed during a pre-trial hearing that Northumbria Police had paid him £10,000 for information about the sexual exploitation of young girls. He said part of his work included going to parties where police suspected girls would be intoxicated and sexually abused. This is pushing the boundaries of acceptability. It is difficult to see any circumstances where somebody with that individual's previous convictions could be approved as a participating informant to go to places where that sort of thing was happening.

The Newcastle case was the biggest child sex investigation since the Rotherham and Rochdale grooming scandals and involved the trial of twenty-five suspects. Putting a child sex offender in contact with children and other sex offenders is a line many police officers would not be prepared to cross. It can be classed as an ethical issue, and there is also the question of the danger to the children from someone who has already been convicted. There is the potential for such men to continue to offend.

Using participating informants is, in itself, highly controversial and there are strict guidelines in place to govern the tactic. The individual should not be encouraged to take part in any serious criminality. There are occasions where participation is appropriate, for instance in the case of a proposed armed robbery. It would be legitimate to allow an informant to drive a stolen car leading up to a robbery, as the police would be able to intervene and arrest the more serious and armed participants.

Using such a tactic is not without risk, therefore, and it would indeed be exceedingly difficult to manage those risks. However, that should not totally rule out the potential to operate in this way, as it can be legitimately claimed that it is being lawfully audacious and is for the greater good.

So in summary, since the so-called bad old days of the 1970s and 1980s, when the system regarding the use of informants became discredited and the Crown Prosecution Service refused to touch any super grass cases, the rules have been tightened considerably. New policies and legislation regarding the use of super grasses, where a participating criminal chooses to give evidence against others in return for a reduction in sentence, have been developed with the introduction of the Serious and Organised Crime and Police Act, known as turning Queen's evidence. This ensured that providing information on a gang or organisation as part of a prosecution case was given an entire legal framework for extracting and using such testimonies. Other legislation governing the use of informants is known as the Regulation of Investigatory Powers Act 2000. The Act's provisions extend to Scotland in cases where a public authority authorises the use of a covert source.

The law is clear that a source has no licence to commit crime. They may, in an authorised operation, infiltrate a criminal conspiracy or be a party to the committing of criminal offences as previously stated. However, this must be within the limits recognised by case law and with the approval of the authorising officer. Acting beyond these limits could lead to prosecution. The need to protect the source cannot alter this.

As I have said, an informant's incentive for informing on others is a potential reduction in a sentence and the prospect of payment. Immunity from prosecution is rarely granted. Detailed negotiations of reductions in sentences are carried out, not by the police but by the CPS, in order to distance officers from the process and reduce the risk of corruption. Inevitably, super grasses will spend the rest of their lives looking over their shoulders, as it is highly likely that their fellow criminals will seek revenge and will look to cause serious harm, if not worse, to the grass. After ending their sentences, these individuals often go into witness protection and assume new identities.

All police forces recognise that covert human intelligence sources are valuable, but they also know that their use carries risks that need to be managed. The National Police Chiefs Council (formerly and at the time known as ACPO – Association of Chief Police Officers) and HM Customs' manual of Standards for Covert Human Intelligence, written in 2004, is held by a police force's Director of Intelligence, normally a detective superintendent, and provides the standards to be adhered to and guidance for all police and customs staff.

So what is the financial cost?

As mentioned previously, informants can get anything from a few pounds for basic information, up to several thousand pounds for helping break up high level organised crime. Payments are typically used to solve, or prevent, crimes including murder, terrorism and serious sexual offences, and can also be made to recover valuable stolen items.

Data revealed in the media, because of a Freedom of Information Act request, stated that forty-one forces in England and Wales collectively paid £19.59m to informants between 2011 and 2016. The Police Service of Northern Ireland spent almost £2m during the same period, while Police Scotland, who only released figures for 2013 to 2016, revealed it had spent £565,248. There are unfortunately no statistics available to show how many convictions happened as a result of paying informants.

The highest spending UK police forces during the period 2011 to 2016 were:

Metropolitan Police - £5,270,659
Police Service of Northern Ireland - £1,995,392
Kent Police - £1,029,145
West Midlands Police - £1,002,834
Lancashire Constabulary - £906,961

Of those who responded, thirty-nine forces in England and Wales provided annual breakdowns, which suggested payments had fallen from £4.1m in 2011-2012, to just over £3.1m in 2015-2016. North Wales Police paid out the smallest amount, handing over just under £40,000 over five years. South Yorkshire Police and Cleveland Police did not provide figures.

More recent figures show that between 2014 and 2019, forces across the police service spent a reduced amount of £13,662,932 on payments to informants. The Metropolitan Police unsurprisingly again spent the most, at £4.3m over the course of the five years. Police Scotland paid the second highest amount, £1.3m during that same period.

Whilst critics stated in the media that it did not stop the ‘cycle of crime’, the National Police Chiefs' Council said that it was ‘a cost-effective tactic’. Considering overall police budgets, such amounts are arguably cost-effective. Provided that the systems are in place to reduce and hopefully eliminate the potential for corruption, the use of informants is a highly productive and legitimate police tactic. And of course, police forces are subject to regular inspections, through not only the HMIC&FRS but also the Office of the Surveillance Commissioner.

In terms of a case study regarding corruption arising from the use of police informants, one of the best cases to consider relates to the former Metropolitan Police officer, Detective Superintendent Tony Lundy.

*Det Superintendent Tony Lundy*

Tony Lundy was most famous for his involvement in the super grass trials of criminals in the 1970s and 1980s and subsequently, his apparent success with his handling of informants.

Throughout the 1970s, the super grass was a tool much feared by criminals. It is generally considered to have started with Bertie Smalls, who, faced with a hefty prison sentence for his part in leading his gang of armed robbers, the so-called Wembley Mob, decided to turn Queen's Evidence against his fellow thieves which resulted in them receiving heavy prison sentences whilst Smalls was granted immunity from prosecution. Although, after the Smalls trial, immunity could no longer be granted, criminals who turned super grass could expect to be rewarded with the super grass tariff, normally a sentence of around five years, most of which would be spent in police custody. Smalls remained in police custody rather than a prison because he continued to provide evidence against other criminals. Indeed, in the following fourteen months, Smalls' evidence convicted a further twenty-one associates for a total of 308 years.

In May 1977, Lundy, then a detective chief inspector, rejoined the Flying Squad. His first success involved an individual named David Smith in September of that year. Smith was involved in a wages snatch in Borehamwood, Hertfordshire, along with George Williams, who too turned super grass. Smith's confession resulted in sixty-nine people being charged, of whom ninety per cent pleaded guilty. Lundy was also involved in the investigation into Harry MacKenny and John Childs, the latter being the first serial murderer in modern times to turn super grass.

The case where it all turned sour for Lundy was brought to public notice in an investigative report in the *Observer*. Two men named Roy Garner and Ken Ross were close associates of criminals, who claimed to have bribed police officers, and of a book maker, David Spicer, alleged to have been a link man for corrupt deals. Spicer was one of a group of people who drank together at two north London pubs, the Torrington Arms and the

Cavalier, and who met at boxing functions and Masonic events. The group included criminals, detectives, and the two men previously mentioned, Garner and Ross. Two of the criminal members of the group, Lennie Gibson and Rudolf Aguda, were already serving ten years for their part in an armed robbery involving the theft of £3.4m of silver bullion in March 1980. Another member of the group was Billy Young, who became an informer and named Garner and Ross as 'fences' (persons who deal in stolen goods) in open court in May 1982. Garner and Ross ran a club in Tottenham called Eltons where Billy Young had worked as a bouncer. A former policeman was the manager. Other officers were regular visitors, as were Spicer, Gibson, Aguda and their associates.

In his statements to police, Young described how Spicer passed cash from himself and other criminals, to corrupt detectives who had supplied information or agreed not to prosecute them. The *Observer* also claimed that another informer called Fred Sinfield had given similar information about Spicer's deals with officers and described how Spicer passed a £10,000 bribe from Sinfield to a senior detective.

At his trial, Spicer said he had often drunk with Garner and Ross and also with DCI Tony Lundy, whom he had known for many years. Tony Lundy was called as a defence witness for Spicer but did not give evidence. Spicer told the court he had often seen Garner, Ross and Lundy together at social events. Spicer, jailed for three years at Snaresbrook Crown Court on 2 June 1982 for conspiracy to steal, was described by Judge Owen Stable as 'a viper who has sunk as low as any human being can'.

Following Spicer's conviction, the then Attorney General, Sir Michael Havers, was asked by the Labour MP Christopher Price to tell the House of Commons what progress had been made on inquiries into his allegations. MPs were also pressing for a progress report on a special internal inquiry into alleged corruption at Scotland Yard. This inquiry was run by Deputy

Assistant Commissioner Ron Steventon and Detective Chief Superintendent Alan Stagg and concerned allegations of corruption around the 1980 silver bullion robbery mentioned previously. It was alleged that these officers had helped to stage the robbery by supplying uniforms, had stolen some of the proceeds and had shared reward money with two associates known as The Bounty Hunters.

Matters rumbled on for years. The following extract from Hansard dated 4 November 1986 once again shows just how far-reaching this issue had become.

HC Deb 04 November 1986 vol. 103 cc810-18103.56 pm

**Mr Clive Soley (Hammersmith)**

I beg to ask leave to move the Adjournment of the House under Standing Order No 10, for the purpose of discussing a specific and important matter that should have urgent consideration, namely, the allegation of serious corruption in the Metropolitan police. It is specific, because I have an official Metropolitan police report, signed by Deputy Assistant Commissioner Steventon, Scotland Yard's most senior anti-corruption officer, that says: 'It is my belief that Mr Lundy' - that is, Detective Superintendent Lundy – 'is a corrupt officer who has long exploited his association with Garner' - that is, Roy Garner. Deputy Assistant Commissioner Steventon goes on to suggest that he believes that Detective Superintendent Lundy should be removed from specialist duty. Elsewhere in the report, Deputy Assistant Commissioner Steventon says that grave doubts must be expressed as to the integrity of Mr Lundy.

Since then, Detective Superintendent Anthony Lundy, Scotland Yard's most senior operational detective, has not only been approved for promotion but has also been appointed to head the new, elite special operations task force that is investigating the international laundering of £26m of Brinks-Mat robbery money. This is equally relevant and important, because the report goes on to say that some of the evidence has been deduced from the silver bullion robbery and the Hatton Garden robbery; in respect of both cases, the report suggests that Garner was not the informant that he was claimed to be and that he was merely exploiting the information that he had received from Lundy. The report continues: The position is further complicated in the case of the Silver Bullion Robbery in that both Garner and Lundy were closely associated with Leonard Gibson, one of the principals convicted of the crime. Photographs have appeared in the press and on television showing all three with other criminals at social functions. The matter is clearly extremely important, because corruption in the police force anywhere must obviously be a serious matter. It is true that the information contained in the World in Action programme was partly available before, in the Brass Tacks programme which the BBC chose not to broadcast, but no legal action has been taken against the World in Action programme.

More information has become available. Even today, I have received information about the names of the two officers who are alleged to have threatened either the careers or the lives of other senior police officers. I do not wish to name those officers at the moment, because first I want to check them out with other sources.

The matter is urgent, because the suggestion, as made in the World in Action programme last night and elsewhere, is that the offences may be continuing. It has been suggested to me that a serious drugs offence has already been partly started but that is not being dealt with in the way in which it ought to be dealt with.

It has been very difficult to get this matter debated. In January 1986, I wrote to the Minister of State, Home Office, who in his reply to me simply said that he did not consider that it was for him to look at these issues. Since then, I have given the Home Secretary the opportunity to take up the matter, but without success.

Therefore, Mr Speaker, I must ask the House to adjourn to discuss this matter, if only to protect the many police officers and members of the public who have approached me and asked me to make sure that it is brought to light and dealt with as an urgent and important matter.

***Mr Speaker***

The Hon Gentleman asks leave to move the Adjournment of the House for the purpose of discussing a specific and important matter that he believes should have urgent consideration, namely, corruption at New Scotland Yard. I listened with great care to the Hon Gentleman, but, as he knows, my only duty is to decide whether this issue should have precedence over the business set down for consideration today or tomorrow. I regret that I do not consider that the matter that he has raised is appropriate for discussion under Standing Order No 10, and I cannot, therefore, submit his application to the House.

Whatever the truth, it is clear that, for a period of years, Tony Lundy was made the subject of a ferocious trial by media. He retired from the Metropolitan Police in 1988 on ill health grounds, suffering from stress.

But this didn't stop the media circus. Billy Young had a supporter in journalist Andrew Jennings, whose book, *Scotland Yard's Cocaine Connection,* in 1991, made serious allegations against Lundy, but Lundy did not respond with legal action. Obviously, the feeling was that 'there is no smoke without fire'.

# GOOD COP, BAD COP

In his book entitled *Lundy,* published in 1992, Martin Short defended Lundy. Short was a British TV documentary producer and author, best known for his exposés on organised crime and Freemasonry. He died in 2020. In his book on Lundy, he stated that, due to his rank, Lundy was in the Superintendents Association, which was not as financially equipped to support Lundy in a costly libel action as traditionally the Police Federation was. He also included a scathing attack on the allegations made by Jennings. He had told Lundy that, if he did unearth positive proof of his corruption, he would publish it without hesitation. This appears not to have happened, even now, all these years later.

Lundy was investigated in October 1994 and the Crown Prosecution Service stated they had found no evidence to prosecute him. Lundy stated that, throughout the investigation, he had not once been interviewed. He sold his story to the *News of the World*, entitled *Bent or Brilliant?* and now resides in Spain.

Writers and indeed many police officers remain divided over this former detective. Was he a great cop or was he 'as bent as a boomerang'? He ran several highly productive informants and certainly used the big-time informant Roy Garner, who eventually went to prison for twenty-two years, to bring to book dozens and dozens of villains. Lundy did speak up for him during Garner's trial, but then again, he would, because he was a top-flight informant. Andrew Jennings claimed that Garner was the 'Top Villain' in London, which Short rubbished. Jennings also claimed that Garner had a 'licence to rob'. In other words, in return for his information, Garner was allowed to act with impunity and at the same time have his pathway cleared through his informing on the competition. Jennings was responsible for the *World in Action* ITV programme in which it was alleged that Lundy was corrupt.

It is the belief of some that what brought Lundy down was being too successful and that this dredged up resentment and jealousy amongst his colleagues. Indeed, John Grieve, a former

Deputy Assistant Commissioner in the Metropolitan Police stated of Lundy, 'His skills were formidable. He was successful and forceful. He clearly had many detractors. He achieved what he set out to do and sometimes annoyed other officers by his single-minded approach to the task in hand. He did not take to either "time servers" or those who, for one reason or another, were unsuccessful. His record as a murder investigator was excellent. His manner was of a man who got results but he did not care who knew it.' *(taken from* Lundy *by Martin Short 1991).*

Certain police colleagues were obviously extremely dismayed by what Lundy was achieving and the methods he was using, but one point that journalist Martin Short made, since ignored by Lundy's detractors, is that nine out of every ten villains he put away admitted to the crimes alleged. This involved the use of villains such as Billy Amies, Maxie Piggott, David Smith and others.

In many respects, it beggars belief what police officers will do to one another, when they are supposed to be on the side of law and order. However, even from the comments of John Grieve, it can be seen why Lundy would have upset some of his apparently less capable colleagues.

The key questions mentioned by Short in his book are these: Was Tony Lundy using Garner legitimately? In other words, was he being used solely to assist the police in apprehending criminals, solving or preventing crime and recovering stolen goods? Or was Garner using an unwitting Lundy not just to gain authorised rewards but to so ingratiate himself with Scotland Yard's hierarchy as to acquire immunity from investigation into his own criminal activities?

Were Lundy and Garner using each other? Was Garner benefiting from rewards, a criminal licence and police intelligence, all courtesy of a conniving and complicit Lundy? Was Lundy receiving not just information enabling him to make huge numbers of significant arrests, but also a cut of Garner's substantial reward payments for which he had nominated Garner? Finally, was Lundy involved in a conspiracy with a man whose crimes were more serious than those committed by those he informed against?

Whether the claims against him were true or false, sadly we will probably never know. Was he a victim of his success with super grasses and informants? Was there a concerted effort made by a number of individuals to unfairly undermine and discredit him? The whole episode was, frankly, totally unsatisfactory from all sides.

This story shows that, in the context of potential corruption surrounding police use of informants, such tactics will always be viewed with suspicion. This is inevitable, bearing in mind that most informants are criminals. That is the very reason why their information is often truthful, albeit, some believe, dubiously obtained. The rules and guidance dealing with how the police should handle sources and their information have become increasingly stringent over the years. This may explain why the figures mentioned previously, regarding payments made to informants, show that reward payments have decreased. Perhaps this is because they are used less. Possibly officers now think that the use of informants is just not worth the risk and the rules governing their use represent a career minefield. If so, then it is a shame because there are occasions when the police still need to be lawfully audacious and the world of informants is, indeed, a murky one!

Another similarly controversial policing tactic involves the deployment of undercover officers. The irony is that arguably, this was never an issue until recent revelations regarding its totally inappropriate and wrongful use.

There are two types of undercover operative:

An undercover foundation operative carries out low level infiltration that does not require the ability to withstand intense scrutiny by people who are potentially suspicious. For example, buying drugs on the street (known as test purchasing).

An undercover advanced operative is trained to undertake deployments involving higher level infiltrations and they must be able to withstand intense scrutiny from anyone who may be suspicious. For example, counter terrorism work.

The public expect law enforcement agencies (LEAs) to use all available powers and tactics to prevent and detect crime or disorder and maintain public safety. There are a few covert tactics available to law enforcement, and undercover policing is one of them. Applied correctly, and supported by appropriate training, it is a proportionate, lawful and ethical tactic which provides an effective means of obtaining evidence and intelligence.

The value of undercover policing as a tactic is essential. Section 26(8) RIPA provides the legal framework for the lawful deployment of undercover operatives (UCOs) as covert human intelligence sources (CHIS). The role of the UCO is voluntary. They are selected, vetted, trained and accredited to gather evidence and intelligence and are deployed under direction in an authorised investigation in which their true identity is concealed from third parties.

LEAs and the communities they serve should value this body of dedicated operatives who carry out this type of work. The role can be dangerous. They are primarily deployed to gather evidence and/or intelligence which is subject to rules under the CPIA (Criminal Procedure and Investigation Act 1996). This Act requires all law enforcement agencies (LEAs) to reveal all relevant material to the prosecutor who has a continuous responsibility to disclose to the defence any material which might reasonably be considered capable of undermining the case for the prosecution, or of assisting the case for the defence.

On the face of it, this would risk exposing the UCOs. However, they carry out their role in the expectation that their identity will always be protected. LEAs, prosecuting authorities and the judiciary have a duty of care to these operatives and there are mechanisms to lawfully protect the identities of sources/informants or the true identities of UCOs.

However, on the back of all this, in 2019, the College of Policing published, for the first time, *Undercover Policing: Authorised Professional Practice*, which is national guidance, for a six-week consultation before the final version was released later that year.

The then College of Policing CEO, Chief Constable Alex Marshall, said, 'Undercover policing is an essential tactic used by police forces to protect the public, save lives and bring serious and organised criminals to justice. The job of an undercover operative is dangerous so any authorisation must be done by an Assistant Chief Constable and any operation lasting longer than twelve months needs to be approved by the Chief Constable. By publishing much of the guidance, withholding only operational tactics which would no longer be viable if shared, we want the public to see the measures we have in place to ensure undercover policing is used in a way that is proportionate, lawful and ethical.'

The guidance sets out clearly the roles and responsibilities of police officers, from those who are deployed on operations to those who supervise and manage undercover officers and authorise operations. It describes the roles of other external scrutiny arrangements, such as the Office of Surveillance Commissioners and the courts.

The guidance has provided an emphasis on the welfare of those working undercover, and foundation operatives now undergo a personality assessment by a psychologist to understand a candidate's motivation and suitability to the role. Advanced operatives undergo a one-to-one psychological assessment with a psychologist or psychiatrist to identify any risk to their wellbeing. The guidance makes it clear that officers themselves, their supervisors and managers all have a role in supporting those who operate in this highly stressful work.

It also refers to the recent issues regarding undercover policing centred on operatives having sexual relationships with individuals they are targeting. The guidance stated that, 'It is never acceptable for a UCO to form an intimate sexual relationship with those they are employed to infiltrate and target or may encounter during their deployment. This conduct will never be authorised, nor must it ever be used as a tactic of a deployment.'

This was the outcome of what occurred during 2010 and 2011, when the UK media disclosed that several undercover police officers had, as part of their 'legend' (false identity and the story behind their deployment), entered intimate relationships with members of targeted groups, in some cases proposing marriage or fathering children with women who were unaware their partner was a police officer in a role as part of their official duties.

Various legal actions followed, including seven women who took action against the Metropolitan Police and the Association of Chief Police Officers (ACPO, now NPCC), in which they stated that they were deceived into long term intimate relationships by five officers. One of these included Mark Kennedy, the first officer to be identified as such.

Kennedy (also known as Mark Stone and Flash) was formerly a Metropolitan Police officer who, whilst attached to the police service's National Public Order Intelligence Unit, (NPOIU), infiltrated many protest groups before he was identified by political activists as an undercover policeman on 21 October 2010. In January 2011, it was reported he had worked as an undercover infiltrator for seven years in the environmental protest movement. During this time, he entered into intimate relationships on false grounds, all of which came to light as part of a systemic pattern of exploitation and manipulation of women in such movements. It also emerged that some other undercover police relationships had resulted in children whose fathers later 'vanished' when their deployment was concluded.

*Mark Kennedy*

Mark Kennedy himself then claimed in turn that he had been incompetently handled by his supervisors and had been denied psychological counselling. It was alleged in *The Guardian* that Kennedy had sued the police for ruining his life and failing to 'protect' him from falling in love with one of the environmental activists whose movement he infiltrated.

Trials of six activists, accused of conspiracy to commit aggravated trespass at Ratcliffe-on-Soar Power Station, collapsed following the revelation of Mark Kennedy's undercover involvement. CPS barrister Felicity Gerry was forced to withdraw the case after Kennedy confessed to the set-up, the evidence of which had been withheld from the defence by the CPS. It was stated that the police were not just observers but acted as agents provocateurs: 'We're not talking about someone sitting at the back of the meeting taking notes - he was in the thick of it.' The CPS also withheld the fact that Kennedy was giving testimony under the pseudonym of Mark Stone and using a false passport supplied by the police. Secret tapes 'that could have exonerated the six activists, known as the "deniers" because they claimed not to have agreed to join the protest' and 'evidence gathered by *The Guardian* now suggests it was the Crown Prosecution Service rather than the police that withheld the tapes'. The CPS lawyer involved in the case, Ian Cunningham, faced dismissal after a report by Sir Christopher Rose criticised Cunningham for failing to ask questions about Kennedy's involvement in the Ratcliffe plot.

The disclosures led to the closure of the units concerned. In 2015, a public inquiry, the Undercover Policing Inquiry, headed by senior judge Lord Justice Pitchford, a Lord Justice of Appeal and member of the Privy Council, was announced. One group representing victims of such practices was the Undercover Research Group, whose website provides alternate coverage and comments on the inquiry.

It was confirmed by the inquiry that undercover police had infiltrated the following groups and movements: Anarchist groups, Animal Liberation Front, Anti-Apartheid Movement, Anti-Fascist Action, Big Flame Black Power Movement, Brixton Hunt Saboteurs, Colin Roach Centre, Dambusters Mobilising Committee, Dissent!, Earth First!, Essex Hunt Saboteurs, Friends of Freedom Press Ltd, Globalise Resistance, Independent Labour Party, Independent Working Class Association, International Marxist Group, International Socialists, Irish National Liberation Solidarity Front, London Animal Action, London Animal Rights Coalition, London Boots Action Group, London Greenpeace, Militant, No Platform, Antifa, Operation Omega, Reclaim the Streets, Red Action, Republican Forum, Revolutionary Socialist Students Federation, Socialist Party, Socialist Workers Party, South London Animal Movement (SLAM), Tri-Continental, Troops Out Movement, Vietnam Solidarity Campaign, West London Hunt Saboteurs, Workers Revolutionary Party, Young Haganah, Young Liberals, Youth Against Racism in Europe.

In November 2015, the Metropolitan Police published an unreserved apology in which it exonerated and apologised to seven women, 'tricked into relationships' over a period of twenty-five years:

> Thanks in large part to the courage and tenacity of these women in bringing these matters to light, it has become apparent that some officers, acting undercover whilst seeking to infiltrate protest groups, entered into long term intimate sexual relationships with women which were abusive, deceitful, manipulative and wrong. ... Firstly, none of the women with whom the undercover officers had a relationship brought it on themselves. They were deceived pure and simple. ... the Metropolitan Police does not suggest that any of these women could be in any way criticised for the way in which these relationships developed.
>
> Second, at the mediation process, the women spoke of the way in which their privacy had been violated by these relationships. It is entirely agreed that it was a gross violation and also accept that it may well have reflected attitudes towards women that should have no part in the culture of the Metropolitan Police.
>
> Third, it is apparent that some officers may have preyed on the women's good nature and had manipulated their emotions to a gratuitous extent. This was distressing to hear about and must have been very hard to bear.
>
> Fourth, it is recognised that these relationships, the subsequent trauma and the secrecy around them, left these women at risk of further abuse and deception by these officers after the deployment had ended.
>
> Fifth, it is recognised that these legal proceedings have been painful, distressing and intrusive and added to the

> damage and distress. Let's make it clear that whether genuine feelings were involved on the part of any officers is entirely irrelevant and does not make the conduct acceptable.
>
> In light of this settlement, it is hoped that the Claimants will now feel able to move on with their lives. The Metropolitan Police believes that they can now do so with their heads held high. The women have conducted themselves throughout this process with integrity and absolute dignity.
>
> *Statement by Metropolitan Police Service, 20 November 2015*

The officers involved had eventually 'vanished', leaving questions and deceit behind, described by the victims as 'psychological torture'. Settlements of £3m for the seven claimants were made as part of the settlement. Eventually, at least twelve women received compensation from the police in the High Court of Justice, though the police avoided making internal documents about the relationships public.

In January 2016, further cases came to light. A complainant stated that they sought disclosure of the cover names of officers who were engaged undercover in this way, and their supervising officers, so that those who had been deceived into relationships, and potentially suffered thereby, would be able to discover the fact. At present, the inquiry is still in progress and the final report not yet completed. Therefore, the sole known impact on police practice is the above statement combined with the alleged disbanding of the units involved.

Kate Wilson, one of the women who had sued the police over her relationship with Mark Kennedy, started a case in 2018 at the Investigatory Powers Tribunal, alleging the police had infringed her human rights in five ways. In documents related to court proceedings, the police admitted that Kennedy's line manager and other officers were aware of the sexual relationship, stating that a 'sexual relationship with [Wilson] was carried out with the acquiescence of his cover officers and line manager'. Previously the police had suggested such relationships were not officially sanctioned.

Therefore, similar to the issue regarding police informants, there are acknowledged risks but the policing consensus is that the tactic, with the right systems and processes in place to retain control, is still valuable and valid. I share this view because there are cases where there is a need to use what are exceptional means in order to deal with the most sophisticated criminals. However, the tactic when used in the cases referred to was like using a sledgehammer to crack a nut. There was no justification in using these means, let alone allowing those undercover officers to behave in the way that they did.

# CHAPTER 7

## What is the impact of police wrongdoing?

It is clear that the main result arising from instances of corruption is that the police will fail to retain public trust in its decision making. It therefore follows that the police service will fail to maintain its legitimacy and will potentially cease to function effectively. The reduction of confidence has dramatic implications for the legitimacy of policing, leading to a reduction in its effectiveness and in the reporting of crimes. This to some extent motivates criminals to continue breaking the law. Consequently, police corruption has a negative impact on law enforcement. As a result, there is a breakdown of co-operation between the public and the police. Therefore, developing a strong ethical standpoint in the police service is essential.

This aspect raises the question of whether corrupt police officers, as servants of the Crown and therefore holding the public's trust, should be punished less than, as much as, or more severely than, other criminals.

Indeed, it is a fact that police officers face ethical challenges in their career and so should be prepared for this challenge. They work in a constantly changing social context and so are exposed to numerous ethical conflicts. It is from this perspective that society should not condemn them forever, without understanding their working environment. However, the public should also understand the risks of engaging in unethical behaviour. Police officers should be punished just like any other criminals but possibly more severely, due to the position of trust they hold.

On the other hand, criminals capitalise on police corruption. As we have seen, criminals can indeed be police officers themselves. They use this opportunity of corruption to shield themselves from potential prosecution. When arrested, criminals can, if the right climate exists, utilise the presence of corruption in the police force. At its most basic, criminals could bribe police officers, and could therefore escape justice as a result. This cycle could ultimately lead to increased criminal activities in society.

From this perspective, police corruption at its most extreme can have a seriously negative impact on law enforcement. As in a case where a police officer tries to cover-up for another officer, it negatively affects the organisation in general and society more broadly. The result of this can be to create a culture of corruption in all levels and departments throughout the organisation.

Police corruption can also demoralise dedicated, hard-working police officers. For example, senior officers who engage in corruption can, at worst, victimise their juniors, who genuinely want to serve the community, into covering up any criminal activity. This culture of corruption may spread to the whole force.

The IPCC (now the IOPC) completed a report covering the period from 2008 to 2011, entitled *Corruption in the Police Service of England and Wales*. This work was commissioned following police involvement in the well-publicised phone-hacking scandal which led to the Leveson Inquiry.

As I have already pointed out, the issue of police corruption has led to a large body of international literature, including official reports, codes of conduct and academic articles. However, there is little information on public views of police corruption and how they think it should be addressed. Public views are important and, in this context, the IPCC report was significant because it was responsible for maintaining public confidence in the police complaints system. In considering how to respond to the Home Secretary's request for a report, the IPCC decided to conduct some new primary research to support its analysis of existing data and case material and undertook both a survey and organised focus groups.

Three key findings emerged. First, though corruption is not at the top of public concerns about crime, where it does exist, it is seen to corrode public confidence and trust in policing. Second, when members of the public were invited to reflect on potential instances of corruption, they were able to provide a nuanced and relatively sophisticated view. Third, there was general acceptance that serious cases required independent investigation, whereas less serious cases could be dealt with locally, although there remained some concerns about police investigating themselves.

Despite the publicity given to alleged police links to the phone-hacking scandal, the findings of the public survey indicated that local crime issues were a greater concern for most people than police corruption. Not surprisingly, when asked for their views about police priorities, survey respondents gave counter-corruption activity a very low rating compared to other issues that they felt impacted on their lives more directly.

In the focus groups, on the other hand, participants did raise police corruption as a concern. Those with negative personal experiences of, and more direct contact with, the police tended to see it as more widespread or even endemic, compared to those with positive experiences and less direct contact. The report highlighted that a survey conducted in 2011 by HM Inspectorate of Constabulary (HMIC) also found that around a third of respondents believed that corruption was a big problem for the police or was common.

Whatever the views about the prevalence of corruption, where it occurred, unsurprisingly, it was held to undermine essential trust.

Most survey respondents were able correctly to identify a series of scenarios as corruption. These included cases ranging from an officer coercing a woman to have sexual intercourse, to senior officers employing a relative, ignoring laid-down recruitment procedures. Grey areas for survey respondents concerned cases where an officer might have been involved in misconduct such as unauthorised disclosure of information. Responses to other lesser incidences - free food and drink from a café or free entry into a night club - were more mixed. However, even here, over half the respondents believed this was definitely or probably corrupt.

The focus groups provided a more sophisticated view of these areas. Corruption was defined by the groups as 'abusing one's power for personal gain'. In the case of excessive force being used against a person arrested, focus groups viewed this as serious misconduct rather than corruption, since it did not involve personal gain. Unauthorised disclosure was also viewed by some as misconduct. Some saw free food or entry as acceptable perks of the job, but others raised concerns that this could be the thin end of a wedge and identified several warning factors, such as regularity and seniority.

When asked to rank six scenarios in terms of seriousness, survey respondents gave top ranking to officers selling drugs they had confiscated; faking evidence against a burglar; and accepting money from a criminal in exchange for information about a case. Those considered less serious involved officers faking arrest figures for a news story; submitting a false expenses claim; and using a warrant card to gain free entry to a football match.

The focus groups provided further insights. Factors that defined seriousness included the seniority of the officer; the frequency of the act; the sums of money involved; the consequences; the presence of intent; the extent to which it involved criminal behaviour; and the number of officers involved.

When asked about who should investigate corruption, both survey respondents and focus group participants made a distinction between serious and less serious cases. The most serious types of case were viewed as requiring some form of external investigation, either by another force or by an organisation independent of the police. The less serious cases were perceived to be the more likely and therefore were viewed as appropriate for handling by local managers or anti-corruption specialists from the same force. An external police force, or an organisation separate from the police, was viewed by focus group participants as providing an unbiased approach and a fairer review of the evidence.

By way of conclusion, the IPCC identified a number of areas for change. These were firstly, the need for clearer information for the public on what constitutes police corruption. The IPCC would, in future, produce a regular analysis of corruption cases it had dealt with, identifying the emerging themes for subsequent publication for public consumption. Next, it required Chief Constables to ensure greater consistency in recording and referring corruption cases to the IPCC. The Commission wrote to Chief Constables, making clear its expectations and the fact this would be reinforced in the Statutory Guidance to be issued following the findings contained within the report. A more effective national system for handling allegations against very senior officers, ie those of chief officer rank (Chief Constable, Deputy Chief Constable and Assistant Chief Constable), was also needed. The IPCC would, in future, work with HMIC, the National Crime Agency (NCA) and the CPS to establish a more formalised and robust system for escalating such complaints. Most corruption allegations would continue to be dealt with by the forces concerned, involving their own Professional Standards and Anti-corruption units. The IPCC would consider whether its oversight of those processes needed to be strengthened, and what resources it would need to do so.

The IPCC concluded that the public expects serious corruption to be investigated by an organisation independent of the police. The IPCC stood, it said, ready to take on more corruption cases if additional resources were made available. Within existing resources, the IPCC would continue to conduct a small but increased number of independent investigations into corruption cases, prioritising those involving senior officers, serious criminal allegations and gross abuse of police powers. The advent of the IOPC did, in fact, see an increase in resources and the additional powers necessary to enable them to conduct the most effective corruption-related investigations. These were in respect of contractors, access to third party data and the power to require the police and other responsible bodies to respond formally to their recommendations.

# CHAPTER 8

## Infamous cases

Some of the cases I am about to detail are not only interesting but also good examples of the breadth of the different forms of police corruption and misconduct.

The first case is perhaps the most notorious and involved what was known as Operation Countryman, an investigation into police corruption in London in the late 1970s. The initial allegations of corruption were made in 1978 by a super grass, who claimed that some officers, including members of the elite Flying Squad which dealt with commercial armed robberies, were receiving bribes from criminals. This was in return for warnings of imminent police raids or arrests, the fabrication of evidence against innocent men, and the dropping of charges against guilty criminals.

It was in August 1978 that officers began investigating these allegations. The unit was initially based at Camberwell Police Station in south London but following attempts to interfere with the team's documents, records and evidence, it moved to Godalming Police Station in Surrey, outside the Metropolitan Police District. It initially targeted officers within the City of London Police but spread to include the Metropolitan Police based at Scotland Yard. Codenamed Operation Countryman because of its use of officers from the so-called 'rural' police forces of Hampshire and Dorset, the investigating team came to be disparagingly known by London officers as 'The Sweedy'. The investigation was ordered by the then Home Secretary Merlyn Rees, and began by examining police activity around three major crimes:

- a £175,000 payroll robbery at the offices of the *Daily Express* in 1976

- a £225,000 robbery outside the headquarters of Williams and Glyn's Bank, London, in 1977
- a £200,000 payroll robbery at the offices of the *Daily Mirror* in 1978. During this robbery, Antonio Castro, a thirty-eight-year-old guard working for Security Express, was killed.

As the investigation proceeded, it began to emerge that the corruption was not limited to 'a few bad apples' within the forces but was 'historically and currently endemic' and 'widespread throughout the hierarchical command rather than confined to those below the rank of sergeant'.

Operation Countryman faced major obstruction from both senior management and lower ranks. Devon's Assistant Chief Constable Leonard Burt told his investigation team not to pass any evidence against Metropolitan Police officers to the Met Commissioner, David McNee. Shortly before his retirement in February 1980, the Chief Constable of Dorset, Arthur Hambleton, Burt's superior, made allegations that Countryman had been wilfully obstructed by Commissioner McNee and Director of Public Prosecutions Sir Thomas Hetherington. In May 1980, Leonard Burt returned to Dorset Constabulary and responsibility for Countryman passed to Sir Peter Matthews, Chief Constable of Surrey, who ordered that all evidence already compiled during the investigation be passed to the Metropolitan Police to be dealt with by their own internal investigation unit.

Much of the investigation's evidence was obtained by police officers going undercover as police officers to infiltrate teams and units suspected of being involved in corruption.

After six years, and at a cost of over £4 million, Operation Countryman presented its findings to the Home Office and the Commissioner. Parts of the report were leaked to the public. It was reported in the media, incorrectly as it transpired, that over two hundred and fifty police officers were forced to resign and many faced criminal charges, after investigations revealed that police membership of particular Masonic lodges formed the nucleus of a criminal conspiracy.

The findings of Operation Countryman have been classified as 'secret' for seventy years and are stored away at the Home Office. The question therefore remains, 'Why was Operation Countryman closed down and made secret for seventy years?'

The official answer has always been that the investigation came to a natural end and corrupt officers had been identified and dealt with. However, the operation had got so big and out of hand that the Home Office started to close it down as it had become an embarrassment to the country. Questions asked in Parliament have, on several occasions, called on different Home Secretaries to release its findings, but such requests have always been refused as these findings are protected by public interest immunity.

It was widely reported that Operation Countryman recommended that the Met Police be disbanded and integrated into neighbouring provincial police forces. Countryman claimed that corruption in the Met went all the way up to Assistant Commissioner level and believed it had enough evidence to prosecute at least three Assistant Commissioners, nine detective chief inspectors, four detective inspectors, twenty-one detective sergeants, and fourteen detective constables.

The investigation team's report actually recommended that over three hundred police officers should be prosecuted. In reality, only eight were ultimately prosecuted and not one of those was convicted. Most of those implicated retired early on the grounds of ill health.

What led up to Operation Countryman represents an example of 'noble cause' corruption with a possible link to other forms. As I previously mentioned, it represents one of the most infamous cases in the history of British policing. The fact that no officers were held accountable represents, in my opinion, one of the darkest periods in policing within this country.

# GOOD COP, BAD COP

The Cardiff Newsagent Three involved three men wrongly convicted of the 1987 murder of Cardiff newsagent Phillip Saunders. He was attacked with a shovel in his back yard and later died in hospital. Michael O'Brien, Darren Hall and Ellis Sherwood spent eleven years in prison before being released.

Their conviction in 1988 was largely based on a confession made by Darren Hall that he had acted as a lookout for the others for a 'robbery that went wrong'. In 1999, the Criminal Cases Review Commission (CCRC) ordered an appeal, during which the unreliability of Hall's 'confession' was emphasised, on the basis that he was suffering from an antisocial personality disorder at the time the statement was made and had since retracted it. The conduct of South Wales Police was also questioned, particularly regarding their interrogations of the suspects.

On 17 December 1999, the Court of Appeal quashed their convictions. Upon their release, Michael O'Brien and Darren Hall announced they would be taking legal action against South Wales Police. They also called for an inquiry into the investigations carried out by the police, pointing to other cases that had recently been overturned on appeal. In 2001, the Police Complaints Authority, as it was known then, stated that no action would be taken against any officers involved in the murder investigation.

O'Brien pursued a civil case against South Wales Police alleging malicious prosecution and misfeasance in public office by police officers. As a result, in October 2006, O'Brien and Sherwood were awarded out of court settlements of £300,000 and £200,000 respectively by South Wales Police, at the time the biggest out of court settlements ever given by an English or Welsh police force. Despite this, O'Brien continued to call for a public inquiry, expressing disappointment that there had been no admission of liability on the part of the police force.

To date, no further action has resulted from the case and no police officers faced criminal charges. The case represents a classic example of 'noble cause' corruption.

It was reported as one of the most brutal murders ever to take place in Swansea. On 14 June 1985, sex shop manager and mother of four Sandra Phillips was sexually assaulted, struck about the head, and eventually strangled. Petrol was sprayed around the Private Shop in Dillwyn Street but was not lit. That was how the shop was found when the area manager arrived just before 2pm and found it closed. It was when he unlocked the door using spare keys and found Mrs Phillips in a pool of blood that a long-running murder inquiry began. Despite exhaustive investigations over several years, and the wrongful conviction and jailing of two men, the brutal murder thirty-four years ago remains unsolved.

Hours after the death, journalists and passers-by gathered as police began their probe. Among them were Wayne and Paul Darvell, two homeless brothers, who lived in hostels by night and drank cider by day. The brothers were well known to the police for petty crimes and were arrested as part of the police investigation. As the questioning continued, Wayne Darvell made a series of confessions, claiming he had been present at the murder and had seen his brother Paul carry it out, although Paul Darvell always maintained his innocence.

The police case centred around Wayne's confession and the fact they had been seen by many people near the shop, with some reporting seeing them with a container which could have had petrol in it. However, despite carrying out forensic tests on the brothers' clothes, they found no traces connecting them to what had been a frenzied attack in the blood-spattered premises.

The brothers were, though, charged with murder. An eight-week-long trial followed and the pair were found guilty and sentenced to life in prison on 19 June 1986, with a recommendation that Paul serve at least twenty years and Wayne fifteen.

Later, an investigation by BBC's *Rough Justice* programme concluded that Wayne's confessions were potentially flawed. He had told police he would take them to the murder weapon but no weapon was found. He showed them a charity collection box he allegedly stole from the shop but it was from a different shop. He also gave details about a St Christopher medal that he said he had taken from the dead woman, but it transpired she didn't have one. It became apparent that Wayne was a serial confessor. His former teacher at a special school said he was forever 'admitting' to things he hadn't done.

It was concluded that there was more than enough evidence to cast doubt on the convictions and, after spending seven years in prison, the brothers were released by the Court of Appeal in 1992.

Albert Kirby, the former head of Merseyside CID, who had led the investigation into the death of toddler James Bulger, reviewed the Darvells' case in 2002. An appeal on the BBC's *Crimewatch* programme threw up new leads and a fresh investigation started in 2004 but was closed five years later. The South Wales Police team completed the recommendations made following the review but stated in 2009 that all lines of enquiry and forensic opportunities had been exhausted. The force apologised for the shortcomings of the original 1985 investigation but said, even though at that point there were no further lines of enquiry to pursue, staff remained fully committed to attempting to bring those responsible for Mrs Phillips' murder to justice.

The two brothers wrongly accused of the heinous crime were later awarded £80,000 in compensation for the time they spent in prison. In March 2005, Paul Darvell, then forty-two, was found dead at his home in what police said was a non-suspicious death.

Once again, this case highlighted the shortcomings of police officers involved in a high-profile case where there is pressure to 'achieve a result'. It is clear in this instance that the first opportunity to arrest, charge and prosecute individuals was taken, rather than the matter being thoroughly investigated. It was noticeably clear that even the most basic of enquiries conducted would have revealed the falsity of Wayne Darvell's confession.

The following case involves one where a senior police officer of the West Yorkshire Police was jailed in January 2019 for 'fitting up' suspects, following a burglary investigation.

Elizabeth Belton, who was a detective chief inspector, was found guilty of conspiracy to pervert the course of justice and sentenced to two years in prison. Her West Yorkshire Police colleague, PC Judith Mulligan, was given a twelve-month prison sentence, suspended for two years, for her role in what transpired to be a conspiracy.

The jury at the trial held at Leeds Crown Court had been told that the pair had plotted to corrupt an identification procedure in an effort to secure convictions against two men. The judge, Tom Bayliss QC, told Belton at the conclusion of the trial that she had 'driven a coach and horses' through police procedures designed to ensure integrity in the justice system. 'The public must be able to trust the police to uphold their rights,' he said. 'How can the public do that when senior police officers are subverting those rights?' These statements demonstrate perfectly the damage that corrupt activity committed by a police officer causes in terms of the relationship between the police and the public. The judge added, 'I think you, Elizabeth Belton, got carried away. You were showing off to your friend and you were throwing your weight around with junior colleagues.'

The corruption took place in September 2013, after two men tried to break into Mulligan's home in the Pudsey area of Leeds. Officers were unable to find any forensic evidence at the police constable's house and the investigation hinged on Mulligan's identification evidence. The officer had first described two teenage suspects wearing dark clothing for the burglary, but officers stopped and arrested two men aged in their thirties. Mulligan later changed her description of the suspects, stating they were older.

The court heard how Mulligan and Belton arranged for photographs to be taken of the two arrested men and sent to

Mulligan prior to the identity procedure. Belton also sent a string of incriminating text messages to Mulligan, boasting about interfering with an investigation, saying, 'You've fit him up lol.' Her texts also described the suspects as 'little shits' and stated, 'They deserve it. I hate burglars.'

The two men charged with attempted burglary were subsequently jailed for twelve months and twenty-eight months. The offence did not come to light until two years after the incident when Belton's text messages were found by a detective constable who was investigating an unrelated case. The prosecution case was that the messages were direct evidence of a plan to corrupt the identification procedure.

The next case involves one which took place in Jersey concerning officers of the States of Jersey Police. It is of personal interest to me because one of those involved, Detective Chief Inspector Charles Quinn, was a guest at our end of course dinner on my initial CID course in 1985. He attended because there was a States of Jersey officer on the course which was the first time such a thing had happened.

At 8am on 18 August 1986, there was a simultaneous dawn raid on the houses of three Jersey policemen. They had been suspended since 1 October 1985, pending an enquiry concerning the conviction of a burglar for theft from a local bookmaker named BJ O'Connor, and were probably imagining that the investigation into their alleged misconduct - fabricating evidence in their pocketbooks - would proceed along more formal lines. Instead, they faced a rude awakening, as their properties were searched and confidential papers seized.

By the start of August 1987, the six-month trial was nearing its end. In the dock were the three accused, Detective Chief Inspector Charles Quinn, Detective Sergeant Barry Follain and Police Inspector Barry Blenkinsop. The charge was conspiring to pervert the course of justice.

At the time, as a young and confident forty-one-year-old Attorney-General, this was one of the highest profile cases that Philip Bailhache had ever prosecuted. Appointed to the role in 1986, he had been working hard preparing the case, even working long hours over weekends. The *Jersey Evening Post* stated that a report collating all the matters and documents relating to the investigation ran to over six thousand pages.

There had been serious problems. Detective Chief Inspector Martyn Le Brocq (Head of the CID) had been identified and dealt with, regarding tampering with pages in his own notebook, but, nonetheless, the expectation was of a successful conviction. One of the documents seized in the raid had also highlighted a rift between Charles Quinn and the Chief of Police David Parkinson, and an accusation was made that part of the motivation behind the case was vindictiveness on his part. But these matters aside, the case seemed to be proceeding smoothly. After all, in early August, the defence had suddenly withdrawn six witnesses, without any apparent explanation. As the *Jersey Evening Post* reported, the Attorney General, in summing up the case for the prosecution, accepted the burden of proving every material particular beyond all reasonable doubt which he was convinced he had done.

But on 6 August 1987, matters went seriously wrong from the prosecution's point of view. After over eight hours of deliberation, the jury returned an unexpected verdict of 'not guilty'. There was, it was reported, an 'audible gasp throughout the Court' at what was an unexpected outcome. It was not a unanimous verdict, and perhaps in a highly unusual attempt to put them on the spot, each juror was required to individually give his or her verdict. However, the result was clear, the case had collapsed, and Charles Quinn was exonerated. The same result was repeated with Barry Follain, while Barry Blenkinsop was cleared unanimously.

The defence applied for costs, and the Royal Court awarded 'substantial' costs to all three police officers. In an unprecedented statement, the States of Jersey Police Associates pledged full support for their Chief Officer, David Parkinson, and divorced themselves from any comments made about his integrity during the trial. Inspector Blenkinsop returned to duty, but Charles Quinn and Barry Follain remained suspended on other matters.

The case had been so demanding and taken so long - over six months - that the Bailiff, Sir Peter Crill, gave the jury an exemption from jury service for ten years.

Senator Ralph Vibert was concerned that Quinn and Follain remained suspended, as he had serious doubts about the motivation and the timing of these charges. On 18 August 1987, he queried why it had taken so long to institute proceedings. He made the point that the number of allegations totalled thirty-seven against Chief Inspector Quinn and twelve against Detective Sergeant Follain. He also stated that most of them related to matters not relevant to the court case and that some charges related to events that took place as long ago as 1981. He further suggested that the additional matters for which the two officers remained suspended amounted to maliciousness because of the 'not guilty' findings by the jury.

In response, Senator John Ellis said that no further charges had been brought and the case was at a stage where the officers concerned had only been informed of the allegations against them. He reported that the issue of timeliness had indeed been raised with the Attorney General and that this resulted in the Attorney General communicating with the Chief Constable of Avon and Somerset, who was overseeing the inquiry, and that things moved ahead at a greater pace from that point onwards.

Senator Ellis also revealed that the total costs incurred by officers from the Avon and Somerset Constabulary for the period 29 August 1985, up to and including 31 March 1987, amounted to £55,225.91 (in the region of £150,000 today).

However, by 25 August 1987, Senator Ellis had decided that his position was untenable. This was because, during the trial, it was revealed he had passed documents to one of the accused officers, Charles Quinn, whom he had known for twenty-five years, which amounted to a clear conflict of interest. In fact, it transpired that the documents had nothing to do with the case in question.

Sadly, this is yet another case where the outcome of proceedings against officers brought no clear conclusion and such instances do nothing to instil confidence in the public regarding the integrity of the police service generally.

The case involving the death of Blair Peach, a New Zealand teacher, was one of the most notorious cases involving the policing of demonstrations and had severe ramifications not only for the Metropolitan Police but for police forces across the UK.

*Blair Peach*

Peach died after an anti-racism demonstration held in Southall. A campaigner and activist against the Far Right, in April 1979 Peach took part in an Anti-Nazi League demonstration in Southall against a National Front election meeting in the town hall and was struck on the head, believed by a member of the Special Patrol Group (SPG), a specialist unit within the Metropolitan Police. He died in hospital that night.

Peach was born in Napier, New Zealand, on 25 March 1946. He emigrated to Britain as a graduate in 1969 and was soon employed as a teacher at the Phoenix Special Needs school in Bow, East London. In 1970 he entered a long-term relationship with a woman named Celia Stubbs, whom he had first met in New Zealand in 1963 when she was visiting the country. Peach helped raise Stubbs's two daughters from her previous relationship, and the couple regarded each other as husband and wife.

Peach was politically active and joined the Socialist Workers' Party (SWP), Socialist Teachers' Association and the local branch of the National Union of Teachers. He was also a committed opponent of racism and was active in the Anti-Nazi League. He had been arrested previously when campaigning on political issues and in 1974 had been charged with threatening behaviour after challenging a local publican's refusal to serve black customers. He was subsequently acquitted.

The Special Patrol Group was formed in 1961 as a specialist squad within the Metropolitan Police. It provided a mobile, centrally controlled reserve of uniformed officers which supported local areas, particularly when policing serious crime and civil disturbances. The SPG consisted of police officers capable of working as disciplined teams to prevent public disorder, target areas of serious crime, carry out stop and searches, or provide a response to terrorist threats. In 1978, there were 204 such officers in the Metropolitan Police Service, divided into six units, each of which contained three sergeants and thirty constables. Each unit was commanded by an inspector. Other forces across the country had available to them variations of the SPG concept but, in the main, these consisted of officers who performed the role at demonstrations as and when required and carried out other policing functions when not so employed.

The use of the SPG proved controversial to some. It was involved in the Red Lion Square disorders, when Kevin Gately, a student demonstrating against a National Front march, was killed by a blow to the head from a blunt instrument. The individual responsible was never identified. Accusations were made that the police were inappropriately violent towards those demonstrating. Some individuals, both inside and outside the police, viewed the SPG with suspicion, seeing it potentially as a force within a force. It has certainly been observed by some that their presence can assume unwanted symbolic significance. It could quite legitimately be argued that on occasions the SPG might apparently solve one problem but in its wake could damage relationships between minority groups and the police in general.

The SPG was disbanded in 1986 and replaced by District Support Units (DSU). After receiving bad press, the DSU were in turn replaced by the Territorial Support Group in January 1987.

In the run up to the 1979 General Election, the National Front announced it was holding a meeting at Southall Town Hall on 23 April 1979, St George's Day. Southall was one of three hundred parliamentary seats where the organisation put up candidates. Prior to the Southall meeting, similar events had resulted in clashes with anti-racist protesters, including in Islington, North London, on 22 April, and in Leicester the next day. At both events, police had been injured trying to keep the two sides separate.

A petition signed by ten thousand residents was raised to cancel the meeting, but to no effect. Ealing Council had blocked previous meetings by the National Front, but on this occasion, they allowed the party to use the hall. Two counter-demonstrations, consisting of a picket on the pavement opposite the hall, and a seated demonstration outside it, were planned. To deal with the potential violence, nearly three thousand police officers were drafted in, ninety-four of whom were on horseback. They arrived at 11.30am and demonstrators began gathering at 1pm in preparation for the 7.30pm National Front meeting.

The number of demonstrators at the town hall rose and included some whom the police considered militants. There were some clashes between police and protesters and a small number of arrests ensued. The police decided to establish a sterile cordon around the town hall, although they still allowed a small, contained demonstration in the High Street. Cordons were set up on Lady Margaret Road, The Broadway, High Street and South Road. Between 2.30pm and 3.15pm, at the High Street cordon, missiles were thrown at the police, who used riot shields to contain the crowd.

According to the official police report, between 5.30pm and 6.30pm, the level of violence rose as the crowd at the High Street cordon again began to throw missiles. About 6.20pm, between five hundred and two thousand protesters tried to breach the police lines. In response, mounted officers were brought in to disperse the crowd. It was believed by some in attendance that the mood changed when the police tactics changed from containment to dispersal. This, it was viewed, triggered the missile-throwing reaction from the crowd.

A house on Park View Road, HQ of People's Unite, was used as a first aid post. The official police report states that the residents were a group of mainly Rastafarians who were squatting at the premises, and that these occupants threw missiles from the house at police in the street. SPG officers entered the house and an altercation broke out in which two officers were stabbed. Those in the house, including those manning the first aid post and those receiving treatment, were struck with truncheons, and an estimated £10,000 of damage was caused to the contents of the house, including equipment for the band, Misty in Roots. The group's manager, Clarence Baker, went into a coma for five months after his skull was fractured by what was believed to be a police truncheon. All those inside were removed from the property, regardless of what they were doing, and there were subsequent complaints by the inhabitants of racist and sexist abuse by the police. Seventy people were arrested either at or near the address. At the trial of one of those arrested, one SPG officer reported that there was no overall direction of police resources at the time and the situation amounted to a free for all.

National Front members began arriving from 7pm. The meeting, it was claimed, was hugely provocative. When it ended at about 10pm, some of the attendees gave Nazi salutes on the steps of the town hall before being escorted to safety by the police.

Once the meeting started, the police allowed the demonstrators to pass along the Broadway towards the crossroads with Northcote Avenue and Beachcroft Avenue. At about 7.30pm, Peach, along with four friends, all of whom had been in the area since 4.45pm, decided to return to their cars and moved along towards this junction. They turned off The Broadway down Beachcroft Avenue, thinking they were heading out of the area, not realising the road only led back to the heavy police cordon at South Road.

At around the same time, two SPG vans, collecting bricks and bottles left behind by the retreating crowd, were both pelted with missiles. A flare or petrol bomb was thrown towards a police coach which, it was alleged, drove through the crowd. No one was injured, but eyewitnesses said that the crowd's mood changed at that point. A police inspector on a building roof radioed to the central control unit that there was what he described as a riot in progress.

The SPG vans of Unit 3 drove to the junction of The Broadway with Northcote Avenue and Beachcroft Avenue to face a group of a hundred to one hundred and fifty protesters. As the officers left the vehicles, they were hit by missiles from the crowd. One officer was hit in the face by a brick which fractured his jaw in three places. The inspector leading the unit radioed that immediate assistance was required.

The official investigation into Peach's death stated that events leading up to this point, while difficult, were relatively straightforward, but conflicting accounts from both public and police muddled what happened next.

The radio call from Unit 3 was picked up by SPG Unit 1, two of whose vans drove into Beachcroft Avenue and stopped at the corner with Orchard Avenue. They came under considerable bombardment from bricks and stones. A police inspector and five constables, who left the first van of Unit 1, were using riot shields, had their truncheons drawn and worked to disperse the crowd. During this action, Peach received a blow on the head. Fourteen witnesses saw it happen and said it was a police officer.

Peach was taken into a nearby house, at 71 Orchard Avenue, after one of the residents saw him being hit. He was given a glass of water but could not hold it. His eyes rolled up to the top of his head and he had difficulty speaking. The residents soon called an ambulance, which arrived within ten minutes, and Peach was taken to Ealing Hospital. He was promptly operated on but his condition worsened and he died at 12.10am on 24 April.

There were an estimated three thousand protesters in Southall on 23 April. Ninety-five police officers were injured, as were thirty-nine of those arrested. Twenty-five members of the public were also injured, of whom Peach was one. A National Front member, found badly beaten near Southall train station, spent two days in intensive care before being released.

The police arrested 345 people but despite police and government statements that outsiders caused the trouble, only two of the 342 charged were non-residents of Southall. Instead of holding the trials locally, they were held twenty-five miles away in Barnet. It was initially reported that ninety per cent of the defendants were found guilty but this figure dropped to seventy per cent once the press began to publicise the matter.

Within a day of Peach's death, Commander John Cass of the Metropolitan Police's Complaints Investigation Bureau began an investigation. Sir David McNee, then Commissioner of the Metropolitan Police, also undertook his own eight-day review of the demonstrations, although he did not include Peach's death as part of his analysis.

On 26 April 1979, the inquest, under the control of John Burton, the West London coroner, opened and was immediately adjourned so that Peach's family could have a second post-mortem done by an independent pathologist. It was again adjourned on 25 May after Commander Cass said his investigation would take another two to three months. By that time, he and his team had interviewed four hundred people.

In early June, after the forensic report stated that Peach was probably not killed by a police truncheon, but by a lead-filled cosh or pipe, a search of the SPG units' lockers found twenty-six weapons, including police truncheons, many of which were unauthorised. These included coshes and knives, as well as sets of keys and a stolen driving licence. The home of one of the constables was also searched and weapons and Nazi memorabilia found, which the officer stated he collected as a hobby.

During his investigation, Cass held several identification parades, as a result of which three officers were identified but no witness managed to identify the man they saw hitting Peach. It later transpired that one officer had shaved off the moustache which he had that day, while it was alleged that the inspector grew a beard and refused to take part in the identity parades. Many of the uniforms that the police wore had been dry cleaned before they were inspected. Cass reported that he had run up against misleading stories from members of Unit 1 and, in his report, claimed that the attitude and untruthfulness of some of the officers involved had clearly obstructed his investigation of what was a serious matter. Cass stated he had identified the individual whom he considered most likely to have hit Peach, but there was insufficient conclusive evidence.

In his 1983 autobiography, *McNee's Law,* Commissioner Sir David McNee stated that all evidence showed that Blair had died from a blow to his skull, almost certainly struck by a police officer.

Cass finished his initial report on 12 July 1979. Thirty investigators had worked for a total of thirty-one thousand hours during the investigation. The report was sent to the DPP, who, while praising the work, stated there was insufficient evidence to justify a prosecution. When the inquest re-opened a week later, both the coroner, Mr Burton, and the lawyers representing the Metropolitan Police were given copies of Cass's report, but both the lawyers representing the Peach family and those representing the Anti-Nazi League were refused copies. The question of whether the family was allowed to view the reports was taken to a Divisional Court, who ruled that as the report was the property of the police, they had the right to withhold it.

Legal counsel for the Peach family requested that the inquest be held in front of a jury, which Burton rejected and the inquest was again adjourned. The High Court rejected a challenge to overturn Burton's decision, which then went to the Court of Appeal_where Lord Denning stated that the inquest should reconvene in front of a jury.

The inquest reconvened on 28 April 1980. The pathologists, one acting for the coroner and the other acting for the family, came to the same conclusions. They believed that the death was from a single blow, not a police truncheon, but a 'rubber cosh' or hosepipe filled with lead shot, or something similar. Both stated that Peach had a thin skull, but not 'pathologically thin'. The action that caused the injury was described as a very severe, single blow.

The inquest closed on 27 May 1980 by which time eighty-three witnesses had been called. However, Burton used Cass's report to determine which witnesses to call and which to ignore. Arguably therefore, it was impossible for anyone to obtain a complete picture of the evidence. A verdict of death by misadventure was given. Many writers have suggested that, given the conclusions of the *Cass Report*, unlawful killing would have been a more appropriate verdict. I would argue that an open verdict would have been the most appropriate. Celia Stubbs, Peach's partner, campaigned for the *Cass Report* to be released and for a full public inquiry. An inquiry was rejected, but in 1989 the Metropolitan Police paid £75,000 compensation to Peach's family.

Following the actions of the police at Southall, the Asian community in the area felt that relations between them and the police had broken down. Many saw the police as aggressors. The matter therefore caused immeasurable damage to police and community relations because no one was ever held to account for Blair's death. In 2010 Andy Hayman, the former Assistant Commissioner for Specialist Operations_at the Met, wrote that Peach's death brought the service and the SPG into disrepute, led to an undermining of confidence in the police and created a distrust of officers that in some quarters, had proved difficult to shake off.

Public reaction to Peach's death, and other underlying racial tensions, including excessive police use of the so-called 'sus law', ultimately led to the 1981 Brixton riots and a public inquiry by Lord Scarman.

Interestingly, and as an aside, as previously mentioned, in 2009 Ian Tomlinson died after he was struck from behind by a member of the Territorial Support Group, the successor to the SPG. The similarities in the deaths proved to be the catalyst for the release of the *Cass Report* to the public. The Metropolitan Police Commissioner at the time of the death of Ian Tomlinson, Sir Paul Stephenson, released the report and supporting documentation. He also offered an official apology to Peach's family.

Since Peach's death, the Met has been involved in a series of incidents and poorly conducted investigations. These include the murder of Stephen Lawrence already mentioned, the death of Jean Charles de Menezes in 2005 and that of Tomlinson, all of which have inevitably tarnished the service's image.

The case of Blair Peach represents a classic in terms of police corruption, ie the 'cover-up'. It is clear from Commander Cass's investigation, that Peach was killed as a result of a blow most likely struck by a police officer. When SPG officers were questioned, they deliberately withheld evidence and information which could have led to the case being resolved. At least one other officer, other than the one who struck the fatal blow, maybe even more than one, knew what had happened.

Why did officers withhold information? Maybe for one of three reasons. First, they knew that unlawful force had been used by the officer striking Peach. Second, the blow was struck using an illegal weapon, ie something other than a police-issued truncheon. Finally, they failed to say what they had seen due to a misguided sense of loyalty. In other words, they closed ranks. Whichever one it was or indeed if it was a combination of the three, their behaviour was reprehensible, to say the least, and reminiscent of the 'Ugly Bus' referred to earlier and the so-called 'Blue Code'.

My final case involves the murder of Lesley Molseed, an eleven-year-old British girl, which occurred on 5 October 1975 in West Yorkshire, England. Stefan Kiszko, an intellectually-disabled young man who lived near the victim in Greater Manchester, was wrongly convicted of sexually assaulting and murdering her, and served sixteen years in prison before the conviction was overturned. Kiszko's mental and physical condition deteriorated while he was in prison, and he died twenty months after his release in 1992, before he could collect money owed to him as compensation for his suffering. His ordeal was described by one MP as 'the worst miscarriage of justice of all time'. Evidence that Kiszko could not have committed the crime was suppressed by three members of the investigation team, who were initially arrested in 1993 before charges were dropped.

Lesley Susan Molseed lived in Delamere Road, Rochdale, Greater Manchester, part of the Turf Hill Estate. Known as 'Lel'

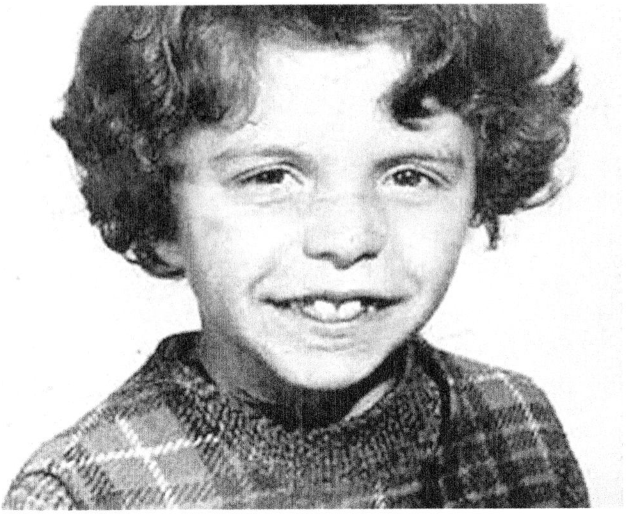

*Lesley Molseed*

to her mother (April), stepfather (Danny), brother, and two sisters, she had been born with a congenital cardiac condition. When she was three, she had open heart surgery, but the procedure affected her health and development, and she remained frail with a reduced mental level for her age.

Around lunchtime on Sunday, 5 October 1975, her mother asked her to go to a shop on nearby Ansdell Road to buy bread and air freshener. The children had a rota for chores and for Lesley, such an errand would have been routine. Walking alone in a blue raincoat, and with £1 in cash and a blue canvas bag, she was last seen by witnesses in secluded Stiups Lane. When Lesley failed to return home, her concerned mother sent her siblings to look for her, with her stepfather also joining the search. At 3pm, with no sign of her, and no evidence that she had arrived at the shops, Rochdale Police were contacted.

A search around the town and the adjacent M62 area was immediately begun. The young girl's body was found three days

*Stefan Kiszko and his mother, Charlotte*

later, around 8am on 8 October, in a natural turf shelf nine metres above a remote roadside layby on the Trans Pennine A672 near Rishworth Moor in West Yorkshire. Lying face down in some tall grass, she had been stabbed twelve times in the upper shoulder and back. Some of the wounds were very deep and one had penetrated her heart. There were no defensive wounds, and a time of death could not be calculated. None of her clothing or possessions had been disturbed, but the money was missing and the offender had ejaculated on her underwear. Other evidence collected by forensic officers included foreign fibres, traces of dry wallpaper paste, and 379 other objects in the vicinity.

At the time of the hunt for Lesley, four girls, Maxine Buckley aged twelve, Catherine Burke, sixteen, Debbie Brown, thirteen and Pamela Hind, eighteen, all claimed that Stefan Kiszko had indecently exposed himself to them the day before the murder. One of them also said he had exposed himself to her a month after the murder, on Bonfire Night.

Kiszko was a twenty-three-year-old tax clerk of Latvian descent. His father, Ivan, had emigrated from Soviet Ukraine and his mother, Charlotte, from Yugoslavia, now Slovenia, after the Second World War, to work in Rochdale's cotton mills. West Yorkshire Police quickly decided Kiszko fitted their profile of the person likely to have killed Lesley, even though he had never been in trouble with the law and had no social life beyond his mother and aunt. His father had died of a heart attack in 1970. Evaluation showed Kiszko had a mental and emotional age of just twelve. He also had an unusual hobby of writing down registration numbers of cars that annoyed him, which supported police suspicions. The police now pursued evidence which might incriminate him and ignored other leads that might have taken them in other directions, a fatal error in any murder investigation.

Acting upon the teenage girls' information and their suspicions of Kiszko's idiosyncratic lifestyle, and having allegedly found girlie magazines and a bag of sweets in his car, the police arrested him on 21 December 1975. During questioning, detectives seized upon every apparent inconsistency between his varying accounts of the relevant days as further proof of his likely guilt. After three days of intensive questioning, Kiszko confessed to the crime. He probably thought that doing so would mean he could go home and that the ensuing investigations would prove his confession to be false. Prior to the Police and Criminal Evidence Act of 1984, suspects did not have the right to have a solicitor present during interviews and the police did not ask Kiszko if he wanted one. His request to have his mother present while he was being questioned was refused and, crucially, the police did not caution him until long after they had decided he was the prime, indeed the only, suspect.

After admitting to the murder, Kiszko was charged on Christmas Eve 1975. Later, in the presence of a solicitor, Kiszko retracted his confession. He was remanded until the trial, which began on 7 July 1976 under Sir Hugh Parkat at Leeds Crown

Court. He was defended by David Waddington QC, who later became Home Secretary. The prosecuting QC, Peter Taylor, became Lord Chief Justice the day after Kiszko was eventually cleared of the murder in 1992.

Kiszko's defence team made significant mistakes. Firstly, they did not seek an adjournment when the Crown delivered thousands of pages of additional unused material on the first morning of the trial. Then there was the inconsistent defence of diminished responsibility, which Kiszko never authorised, on the grounds that the testosterone he was receiving for his hypogonadism might have made him behave unusually. Kiszko's endocrinologist strongly disagreed with this theory, and if called to testify, would have said that his treatment could not have caused him to carry out a murder. He was never called.

The manslaughter defence, known in legal parlance as 'riding two horses', clearly undermined Kiszko's claims he was totally innocent and destroyed his alibis. In fact, his innocence could easily have been demonstrated. The pathologist who examined Lesley's clothes found traces of sperm, whereas the sample taken from Kiszko by the police contained no sperm. Kiszko had broken his ankle some months before the murder and, in view of that and his being overweight, he would have found it difficult to scale the slope to the murder spot. The sperm findings were suppressed by the police and never disclosed to the defence team or the jury. Neither was the medical evidence of his broken ankle.

Kiszko gave evidence that, in July 1975, he had become ill and been admitted to Birch Hill Hospital, where he was given a blood transfusion. In August 1975 he was transferred to a Manchester hospital and diagnosed as being anaemic and with a hormone deficiency. He agreed to injections to rectify the latter problem and was discharged in September 1975. He said that he had never met Lesley, claiming he was with his aunt tending his father's grave in Halifax at the time of the murder, before visiting a garden centre and then going home. When asked why he had confessed,

Kiszko replied that he started to tell these lies which seemed to please the interviewing officers and that eased the pressure on him. He thought that, if he admitted to the killing, the police would check out what he had said, find it untrue and would then let him go.

His conviction was secured by a ten to two majority verdict on 21 July 1976 after five hours and thirty-five minutes' deliberation. He was given a life sentence.

After a month in Armley Prison, Kiszko was transferred to Wakefield Prison and as a convicted sex offender, was immediately placed on Rule 43 to protect him from other inmates. He was fiercely and bitterly hated by most inmates, receiving taunts and several verbal and written death threats during his first months in prison and was physically attacked four times. On 24 August 1976, just after being transferred to Wakefield Prison, he was set upon in his cell by five prisoners who stole his watch, smashed up his radio, cut his mouth and injured both his leg and ankle. The attackers said they did it for Lesley and her family. On 11 May 1977, he was hit over the head with a mop handle, leaving him in need of three stitches. In December 1978, he was punched in the face by another prisoner in an unprovoked attack, whilst in the prison chapel. In March 1981, he was again punched in the face by a prisoner whilst in the prison yard, but this time Kiszko fought back. Blows were exchanged and a fight broke out. The two had to be separated by guards. Both men were given a loss of privileges for twenty-eight days.

On each occasion, the attacks on Kiszko earned him absolutely no sympathy, from either other prisoners or guards. He was not physically attacked or threatened again during his remaining eleven years in prison. During much of that time, he was in the hospital wing of prisons. When he was not, he was placed among less violent offenders.

Kiszko launched an appeal, but it was dismissed on 25 May 1978, when Lord Justice Bridge said that the appeal judges could find no grounds whatsoever to condemn the jury's verdict of murder as in any way unsafe or unsatisfactory.

In July 1979, the Inland Revenue finally wrote to Kiszko to inform him he had been sacked and from late 1979 onwards, Kiszko developed schizophrenia and began to suffer from delusions. One of these was that he was the victim of a plot to incarcerate an innocent tax office employee so the effects of imprisonment could be tested on him. Over the next decade, any of Kiszko's claims of innocence were labelled as symptoms of his schizophrenic delusions or attributed to his being in a state of denial.

In October 1981, Kiszko was put on the punishment block for possessing scissors in his cell. On 11 November 1981, he was transferred to Gloucester Prison. In April 1983, he was told he would only ever be eligible for parole if he admitted to the murder. If he continued to deny being a child killer, then he would spend the rest of his natural life behind bars, but this made no difference to Kiszko's stance. Thirteen months later, while still denying having carried out the murder, he was moved to Bristol Prison. Such was his mental deterioration that a month later, in June 1984, it was recommended by a forensic psychiatrist that he should be moved to either Broadmoor, Park Moss Side Hospital (later Ashworth Hospital, Liverpool) or Rampton, but nothing came of it. Six months later, in December 1984, Kiszko was returned to Wakefield Prison.

In August 1987, he was transferred again from Wakefield to Grendon Underwood Prison, where, in June 1988, the prison governor tried to persuade him to enrol on a sex offenders treatment programme, in which he would have had to admit to Lesley's murder. This would have led to him having to discuss what had motivated him. Kiszko refused to take part and repeatedly refused to address his so-called offending behaviour, on the grounds that he had done nothing that needed addressing. He left Grendon Underwood in May 1989, where he was classed as having made no progress, and moved back to Wakefield Prison. In July 1990, he said he was striking out a ghost who was trying to sexually abuse him. Finally, on 15 March 1991, Kiszko was transferred to Ashworth Hospital, under Section 47 of the Mental Health Act 1983, after six months' delay, on the grounds of his deteriorating mental health.

Kiszko's mother continued to profess her son's innocence but was ignored and stonewalled both by the legal system and by politicians, including, somewhat ironically as we now know, her local MP Cyril Smith, and Prime Ministers James Callaghan and Margaret Thatcher. As regards Cyril Smith, after his death, numerous allegations of child sexual abuse were made against him, and many made during his lifetime re-emerged. In 1984, Kiszko's mother contacted JUSTICE, the UK human rights organisation which investigated many miscarriages of justice. Three years later, she was put in touch with solicitor Campbell Malone, who agreed to look at the case.

Malone consulted Philip Clegg, who had been Waddington's junior at the July 1976 trial. Clegg had expressed his own doubts about the confession and conviction at the time, and over the next two years, Clegg and Malone prepared a petition to the Home Secretary. The draft was finally ready to be sent on 26 October 1989. On the same day, David Waddington was appointed Home Secretary, before resigning in November 1990 to take up a peerage and to serve as Leader of the House of Lords. He was replaced by Kenneth Baker.

In February 1990, the Home Office privately disclosed that Kiszko's first parole hearing would take place in December 1992, by which time he would have served seventeen years in custody. However, he would only be released if he admitted to having murdered Lesley and if he could convince the Parole Board that he would not be a danger to children or the public.

In February 1991, Campbell Malone, with the help of a private detective named Peter Jackson, finally persuaded the Home

Office to reopen the case, which was then referred back to West Yorkshire Police. During his research, Jackson found someone who confirmed that Kiszko had been seen with his aunt tending his father's grave on the day the murder took place. They said they could not understand why they had not been called to give evidence at the trial. Someone else said that Kiszko had been in a shop around the time of the murder.

Apart from the witnesses found by Jackson, West Yorkshire's Detective Superintendent Trevor Wilkinson, assigned to the case, immediately found several glaring errors. Existing medical evidence proved conclusively that Kiszko was innocent. He had male hypogonadism, which rendered him infertile, contradicting forensic evidence obtained at the time of the murder. In 1975, his testes had measured four to five millimetres, whereas the average adult testicular size was fifteen to twenty millimetres.

Also that month, the four girls, now aged twenty-seven, twenty-eight, thirty-one and thirty-three, who were involved in the original court trial, admitted that their evidence, which had led to Kiszko's arrest and conviction, was false, and that they had lied for 'a laugh' and because 'at the time it was funny'. Catherine Burke, interviewed on 14 February 1991, said she had not thought it would go as far as it did. She said she went along with what Pamela Hind said. Maxine Buckley said it was not Kiszko who had exposed himself to her, but she had seen a taxi driver urinating behind a bush on the day of Lesley's murder. She also refused to apologise. Debbie Brown refused to make any statement. Hind was a friend of Lesley's older sister but she was the most remorseful of the four, saying that what they did was 'foolish but we were young' and that, had she appeared in court, she would have told the truth about Kiszko, unlike her three friends, who had all committed perjury. She herself did not think Kiszko would be convicted. A decision was made by the prosecuting authorities for a senior police officer to caution Pamela Hind and Catherine Burke for the criminal offence that each had undoubtedly committed. No further action took place against Buckley and Brown as they made no admissions of guilt and there was no other evidence to pursue a case against them.

In August 1991, the new findings in Kiszko's case were referred to Home Secretary Kenneth Baker, who immediately passed them to the Court of Appeal. On 19 December 1991, Kiszko was moved from Ashworth to Prestwich Hospital.

On 17 February 1992, ten months before his parole hearing, the judicial investigation into Kiszko's conviction began. It was heard by three judges, Lord Chief Justice Lane, Lord Justice Rose and Mr Justice Potts. Present at the hearing were Franz Muller QC and William Boyce for the Crown, who were there to argue that Kiszko was guilty of murder and therefore must remain in prison custody for at least another ten months until the parole hearing. The defence case was put by Stephen Sedley QC and Jim Gregory. After hearing the new evidence presented by Sedley and Gregory, Muller and Boyce did not put up any contrary argument and immediately accepted its validity.

After hearing the new evidence, Lord Chief Justice Lane stated that it had been shown that Kisko could not produce sperm and that, as a result, Kisko could not have ejaculated over the girl's knickers and skirt, and therefore, consequently could not have been the murderer. Kiszko was cleared and Lord Chief Justice Lane ordered his immediate release from custody. The 1976 trial judge Sir Hugh Park, who had praised the police and the thirteen-year-old girls at the original trial, apologised for what had happened to Kiszko but said he was not sorry for how he had handled the court case. Anthony Beaumont-Dark, a Conservative MP, said, 'This must be the worst miscarriage of justice of all time. It brings shame on everyone involved in the case' and demanded a full, independent and wide-ranging inquiry into the conviction.

The Molseed family, who were totally convinced of Kiszko's guilt up to the very moment of him being cleared, also publicly apologised for the things they had said after his conviction, such as demanding that he be hanged in public. Indeed, Lesley's stepfather, Frederick Anderson, had hurled a volley of angry verbal abuse at Kiszko's mother, Charlotte, outside the court after her son was convicted. Anderson had also told the media that he would be outside the prison gates waiting for Kiszko, should he ever be released.

After the Court of Appeal's decision, Kiszko's mother said that it was David Waddington who ought to be 'strung up' for his pro-capital punishment views and for the way he had handled her son's defence in 1976. Lord Chief Justice Lane himself, David Waddington, Sheila Buckley, Maxine Buckley, Hind, Brown and Burke and prosecution barrister Peter Taylor all offered no apology, nor did any of them express any words of remorse or regret for what had happened. Even the West Yorkshire Police, while accepting and admitting that they had been wrong, tried to justify the position they had taken. All Waddington would say was that, if this evidence had been available in July 1976, the trial would have taken a vastly different course. However, the evidence was always available. It was just that so many failed to look for it!

Dick Holland, the surviving senior officer in charge of the original investigation, did apologise, stating that no words could express the regret he felt for the family and for Kiszko. He tried to claim that the original investigation had been carried out diligently and honestly within the terms that were legally and scientifically available. He went on to say that after Kiszko's arrest, the forensic science service had received a handkerchief which may have had seminal fluid on it from Kiszko. He stated that after his arrest, Kisko had produced a sample in the presence of his solicitor and doctor, which was sent to the laboratory for comparison and therefore this evidence should have been followed up by the defence. Holland was just another individual, trying to absolve himself of blame.

On 2 March 1992, Dr Edward Tierney, who ordered the sperm tests that led to the freeing of Kiszko, was dismissed after twenty-five years because he had demanded that police surgeons should be independent of the police and Crown Prosecution Service.

Kiszko needed further psychiatric treatment and remained in Prestwich Hospital until late April 1992 when he was finally released, but the sixteen years of incarceration for something he had not done had both mentally and emotionally destroyed him. Kiszko became a virtual recluse and showed little interest in anything or anyone. He bought a new car, a silver Ford Sierra, and drove it on short journeys to the shops or garden centres or to visit relatives, but other people's apologies for what had happened, and any encouragement and support, seemed to frighten him.

As his mental health had deteriorated over the years, so had his physical health. In October 1993, he was diagnosed as suffering from angina. He died at 1am on 23 December 1993, after suffering a massive heart attack, at his home, eighteen years and two days after he made the confession that helped lead to his wrongful conviction for murder. Lesley's sister was one of those who attended his funeral two weeks later, on 5 January 1994. His mother Charlotte died four months later, at Birch Hill Hospital, Rochdale, on 3 May 1994, at the age of seventy. The two are buried together in Rochdale Cemetery.

After release from prison, Kiszko had been told he would receive £500,000 in compensation for the years he had spent in prison. He had received an interim payment, but neither he nor his mother ever received the full amount since both died before Kiszko was due to receive it.

In 1994, the senior officer in charge of the original investigation, Detective Superintendent Dick Holland, and the retired Forensic scientist who had worked on the case, Ronald Outteridge, were formally charged with 'doing acts tending to pervert the course of justice' by allegedly suppressing evidence in Kiszko's favour, namely the results of scientific tests on semen taken from the victim's body and from the accused. On May Day

1995, the case was challenged by defence barristers, arguing that the case was an abuse of process and that charges should be 'stayed' as the passage of time had made a fair trial impossible. The presiding magistrate agreed and as the case was never presented before a jury, the law regards the accused as presumed innocent.

Holland, who came to public prominence as a senior officer on the flawed investigation into the murders committed by the Yorkshire Ripper, had retired in 1988, at a time when he viewed the conviction of both Kiszko and of Judith Ward, whose conviction was also later viewed as unsafe, as being among his finest results during his thirty-five years in the police service. However, Holland was demoted during the Yorkshire Ripper Inquiry four years after Kiszko's conviction. He died in February 2007 at the age of seventy-four.

The hunt for Lesley's real killer continued. In 1985, with the case closed and the public and the police all believing that Lesley's killer was safely behind bars, her clothes, taken from the crime scene, had been destroyed but strips of adhesive tape, used to remove fibres from her semen-stained knickers, had been kept. Scientists from the Forensic Science Service's lab in Wetherby, West Yorkshire, managed to extract sperm heads from this tape. From these sperm heads, in 1999, for the first time ever, a DNA profile of the man who killed Lesley was obtained. However, he wasn't on the National DNA Database and so the case once again stalled.

In September 2005, fifty-three-year-old Ronald Castree was arrested in connection with another sex attack, with which he was never charged. A DNA sample, taken from him in connection with this arrest, was automatically run through the National DNA Database, where it produced a direct match to the semen sample found on Lesley's underwear.

Castree was charged with Lesley's murder in November 2006 and made his first court appearance on 7 November where he was remanded in custody. At a court hearing on 19 April 2007, Castree pleaded not guilty and was refused bail.

Born on 18 October 1953 in Littleborough, and originally from the Turf Hill estate in Rochdale where Lesley had lived, Castree, a comic book dealer, lived in nearby Shaw and Crompton and was a taxi driver for many years. He was unpopular with his neighbours, who said he had a very nasty temper. In September 1975, two weeks before Lesley's murder, Castree's wife had given birth to a son, although Castree was not the baby's biological father. On 3 October, she went back into hospital with deep-vein thrombosis and remained there for a week. This left Castree home alone on the day of the murder. The birth of the child may have been a trigger for Castree's murder of Lesley. He and his wife had two more children together, but they split up in 1996 and divorced a year later. On 3 July 1976, eight months after Lesley was killed, Castree abducted and sexually assaulted a nine-year-old girl. He pleaded guilty and was fined £25 on both counts of indecent assault and incitement to commit an act of gross indecency. In July 1978, he was again fined £50 after indecently assaulting a seven-year-old boy.

Castree's trial for Lesley's murder began at Bradford Crown Court on 22 October 2007. During his trial, a scientist told the jury that the chances of the semen samples on Lesley's knickers belonging to anyone other than the defendant were one in a billion. Castree was found guilty and jailed for life, with a recommendation he should serve a minimum of thirty years, which is expected to keep him in prison until November 2036 when he will be eighty-three years old.

Unfortunately, the case of Stefan Kisko is another example of misconduct or corrupt behaviour on the part of the police officers involved. I have provided great detail about this case, in an effort to show how the corrupt behaviour of police officers can, at worst, destroy people's lives. Even if not overtly corrupt, at the very least in this case, there existed a failure to investigate Lesley's murder thoroughly. Once Kisko became a convenient suspect, all other possibilities were ignored and efforts made to withhold evidence from the defence which would have shown that Kisko could not possibly have committed the murder. The appalling conduct of the police officers involved was compounded through the inadequacies and laziness of the lawyers involved in the original case, both prosecutors and those acting for the defence.

What will have become apparent to the reader is that most of the serious cases used, both in this chapter and elsewhere within the book, are historic. Does this tend to suggest, therefore, that serious police corruption and misconduct are a thing of the past? Does it mean that the mechanisms now in place ensure that opportunities for bad behaviour by police officers are less and that there is a greater deterrent effect? Does it mean that police officers are naturally better behaved nowadays?

The final chapter will challenge this potential viewpoint and looks to discuss the future and what appears to be the trend in relation to today's serving police officers in terms of misconduct and corruption.

# CHAPTER 9

## What does the future hold?

As policing has developed in this country, so awareness that police officers, as human beings, may be susceptible to corruption and misconduct, has increased. This is reflected in the developments of measures to counter the problem. It was the Police Act of 1964 which incorporated, for the first time, a formal disciplinary code. Since that time, as I described earlier, there have been considerable modifications of those early measures, leading to the current Police Code of Ethics.

I wrote at the end of the last chapter that many of the very worst cases of the more traditional types of police corruption now appear very dated. I suggest that this reflects change. The moral compass of the vast majority nowadays is vastly different to what it was during the middle of the last century. People, and therefore police officers, are less influenced through financial incentives, which, in the context of this book, relate to the receipt of bribes.

In a similar vein, clear evidence suggests that individuals, and again therefore police officers, are less likely to fall foul of so-called 'noble cause' corruption motives. Perhaps this is because individuals today are less inclined to risk their livelihoods by breaking the rules or perhaps morals are higher today than many years previously? As regards the 'noble cause' issue, there seem today to be fewer occasions where groups of officers are involved in corrupt activities.

However, what is clear is that the types of police misconduct have changed. The Code of Ethics, as the name suggests, tends to focus on the ethical dilemmas facing the modern-day police officer, albeit that, in its broadest terms, the Code still incorporates pretty much all that the various disciplinary codes did previously. A greater emphasis is now placed on peers to address misconduct witnessed by them, rather than just supervisors and managers. We appear to have entered the era of the whistleblower. This brings its own issues and problems. It can become a means to resist management and leadership through spurious reporting. There is also the issue that, having encouraged so-called whistleblowing, there is now an expectation that any and all allegations will be investigated, no matter how frivolous. Similarly, it is believed by some to pander to those who wish to pursue a 'politically correct' agenda, which leads to an outright fear developing within the workplace. Individuals have become afraid to use so-called banter or tell jokes for fear of upsetting someone who then decides to formally report the incident. There does appear to be a greater emphasis therefore on internal behaviour, rather than on how officers are performing their duties. Whilst this is my opinion, I am well aware that many others feel the same and there are genuine concerns that such agendas are breeding a quite different police service, one less focused on crime fighting and providing a service to the public.

So where does this leave the discussion as regards the issue of corrupt behaviour? In addition, what are the current trends regarding police misconduct?

One area of real concern supported by statistics is the increased number of officers abusing their position in relation to sexual misconduct. Such abuse can have serious implications for the public's view of policing, and the trust of the police as an institution.

A review of police sexual misconduct in the UK by HM Inspectorate of Constabulary revealed on average 218 cases a year between 2014 and 2016, or around one case per 1000 officers. A follow up report from last year shows 415 cases over the following three years, an average of around 138 a year. Such cases are fortunately still relatively rare. However, in many cases, the officer's actions can re-victimise those who are already victims of domestic abuse or rape. Perhaps unsurprisingly, it seems that these sorts of cases do lead to this form of misconduct. Such abuse of position is also likely to be under-reported, with victims fearing they will not be believed.

Compared to other forms of police corruption, sexual crimes by serving officers are under-researched, with most of the existing research focusing on the US and Canada. However, I came across some research carried out by a PhD student and serving police officer named Fay Sweeting. She has explored the scale of the problem in England and Wales and has then considered what forces could be doing better to tackle the issue. She makes reference to the case of PC Stephen Mitchell of Northumbria Police who was jailed for life in 2011 for two rapes, three indecent assaults and six counts of misconduct in a public office, having targeted some of society's most vulnerable for his own sexual gratification. The case prompted an urgent review into the extent of police sexual misconduct and the quality of internal investigations. One of the recommendations required forces to publicly declare the outcome of misconduct hearings.

In an analysis of documents from 155 police misconduct hearings, Faye identified the following different behaviours.

Firstly, voyeurism, by, for example, using a police helicopter camera to observe women bathing topless in their private gardens. Next come sexual assaults, relationships or attempted sexual relationships with victims or other vulnerable persons. While the national figures show some 117 reports of sexual assaults by police officers, the misconduct hearings studied featured primarily cases of professional malpractice through consensual but inappropriate relationships that fell below the threshold of criminal behaviour.

Another evolving issue involves sexual relationships with offenders. Similarly, while the data was heavily sanitised for publication, only a very small number of cases involved assault. In most cases, these were consensual relationships, albeit inappropriate ones, taking into account an officer's position. There were cases of sexual contact involving juveniles, including making or distributing pornographic images of children.

The next prevalent case type involved issues regarding behaviour towards other police officers, including sexual assaults on colleagues and sexually inappropriate language or behaviour. There were cases involving sex on duty, chiefly between colleagues and work partners. There were also cases involving unwanted sexual approaches to members of the public, such as pressuring a member of the public, who is not a victim or witness, for their phone number and then sending sexually inappropriate messages.

The final type of cases identified involved pornography, such as posting intimate images of former partners on revenge porn sites and, in one case, using a police camera to record a pornographic film.

The most common type of sexual misconduct was officers having sexual relationships with witnesses or victims, accounting for nearly a third of all cases. Many of these victims had histories of domestic or substance abuse, or mental illness, making them highly vulnerable. Interestingly, the victims revealed many of the same risk factors as those found in people targeted by sex offenders. There are also similarities between the actions of these police officers, compared to those carried out by prison officers or teachers who are also more likely to select victims they believe are easily controllable and less likely to speak out.

It was found that the second most common type of misconduct involved the way police officers treated their colleagues. It such cases, it was more often a high-ranking male officer towards a junior or less experienced female officer. Generally, higher-ranking officers have less contact with the public and more contact with staff, which, the researcher suggests, may at least partially explain this finding.

Perhaps unsurprisingly, it was found that most officers

involved in sexual misconduct were male. Interestingly, for the handful of female officers in the sample, almost all cases involved sexual relationships with offenders.

From the research, it was apparent that the hearing documents did not provide in depth information, and in media coverage, such as that involving the case of PC Tara Woodley, who helped her sex offender partner evade police, it is perhaps harder to understand who held the power and control in such relationships, ie is it the male offender exercising power in an effort to achieve an outcome?

Interestingly, and for no apparent reasons, the outcomes of sexual misconduct hearings differed. There were geographical differences, with officers more likely to be dismissed for having sex with victims in forces from the south of England than in the north, while officers having sex on duty were more likely to be dismissed in the Midlands. Officers above the rank of sergeant were more frequently dismissed than constables, suggesting there is less tolerance of misconduct for those of higher rank. In terms of trends, it does seem to be the case that, in recent times, there has been an increased number of reports and investigations of corruption involving individuals of chief officer rank. It is interesting that the research compared this to similar cases in the NHS, where nurses involved in sexual misconduct are more likely to be struck off than doctors.

The findings suggest that police forces in England and Wales are taking sexual misconduct seriously, with ninety-four per cent of all cases leading to formal misconduct actions, and seventy per cent leading to dismissal. However, as previously mentioned, the variation of outcomes across the country is a concern, and there is evidence of misconduct hearing panels not following the College of Policing Guidance as to how such matters should be dealt with.

Despite these outcomes, it is interesting to note that the HM

Inspectorate of Constabulary's (HMIC&FRS) report from last year argues that police forces are not moving quickly enough to deal with the issue, citing lack of investment, training and poor record keeping. There can be no place in the police for those who would abuse their position. However, I will later discuss the numbers of officers and staff currently deployed to Professional Standards Departments and I feel that a lack of investment in terms of adequate resourcing is not necessarily the case.

Here are brief details of cases reported on by the IPCC in 2011.

A Northumbria police constable, mentioned briefly at the start of this chapter, was convicted of two counts of rape, three indecent assaults and six counts of misconduct after he stood trial at Newcastle Crown Court, following an investigation conducted by Northumbria Police's PSD and managed by the IPCC. The investigation found that the officer used his position to assault women. The trial heard that he targeted vulnerable women, including heroin addicts and shoplifters, by offering to help them whilst they were in custody at Newcastle's Pilgrim Street police station. He then asked them for sexual favours. It was also established that the officer used police databases to trace potential victims. Victims showed great courage in coming forward, giving overwhelming evidence against the officer, and he received a sentence of life imprisonment.

In 2007, an investigation was conducted by South Wales Police's PSD, supervised by the IPCC, which identified links between a retired detective chief superintendent who had established his own business and a retired detective constable who had rejoined the force as a civilian administrator. The police investigation showed that whenever the detective chief superintendent's company took on a new client, the other retired officer would undertake checks on the police computer systems, to provide information such as addresses, vehicles owned and any criminal record details, in order to assist the retired officer's investigations. The investigation also established that the force administrator had links with a known criminal. That association led to investigations into money laundering, following the seizure of over £200,000 from the administrator's house when his premises were searched on his arrest for the unauthorised disclosure of information. Following a successful prosecution, the retired detective chief superintendent was sentenced to eighteen months' imprisonment and the force administrator received four years' imprisonment.

In March 2010, the IPCC undertook two investigations into allegations of irregularities in a North Yorkshire Police recruitment exercise. The allegations involved the Chief Constable, Deputy Chief Constable, a police constable and two members of Human Resources (HR) staff. HR staff were alleged to have used their position to help both themselves and their acquaintances to progress in the recruitment exercise, while the police constable was alleged to have assisted Police Community Support Officers (PCSOs) in the same way. This investigation resulted in the two members of HR and several other staff being dismissed, while the police constable received a final written warning. An independent investigation was conducted into the allegation that the Chief Constable and the Deputy Chief Constable jointly assisted a relative in circumventing the first stage of the recruitment exercise and the further allegation that the Chief Constable had also assisted a member of his extended family. As a result, the Deputy Chief Constable faced a misconduct meeting, while the Chief Constable faced a gross misconduct hearing. This was the first time for thirty-four years that a serving Chief Constable had faced such a hearing. The Deputy Chief Constable's hearing in December 2010 found he had breached the Code of Conduct on two counts in that he failed to challenge and report improper conduct and thus was guilty of discreditable conduct. He received management advice. The Chief Constable admitted gross misconduct on the opening day of his hearing in May 2011 and received a final written warning.

In October 2008, a serving member of South Wales Police became involved in a criminal conspiracy with three other men, which involved attempts to blackmail two local businessmen. The first case involved threats to an individual who was under surveillance in respect of drug dealing. He was told that unless he paid £30,000, evidence would be given to the police that would support the case of drug dealing. At the same time, the officer was involved in another plot to obtain £24,000 from a businessman who had previously been the victim of a robbery, during which his family were tied up by the offenders. The businessman was contacted by an accomplice of the officer, who informed him that he would be the subject of another robbery. The accomplice offered to provide protection, including the services of a 'bent' police officer with firearms experience. The businessman met the men offering the protection and the police officer and during the meeting, the police officer produced a handgun. Following the investigation, the police officer was arrested, and eventually admitted his involvement. He subsequently agreed to provide evidence against his co-conspirators. Whilst on bail for the offences, he was dismissed from the police. At a criminal trial, he received four years' imprisonment.

Two Cheshire Constabulary officers were investigated for breaches of policies and procedures in relation to their dealings with a prison inmate. On 31 January 2008, the two detective constables collected the man, who was on remand at HMP Altcourse, with the intention of attempting to clear up unsolved car crime in the Nantwich area. It was alleged the prisoner was given a list of offences to admit to and was then allowed to meet his girlfriend. It was further alleged that the prisoner brought drugs and a mobile phone back into HMP Altcourse. Activity around the prisoner's cell following his return raised suspicions with staff there. These concerns were relayed to Cheshire Constabulary and the matter was referred to the IPCC. Their investigators interviewed a number of people, including inmates at HMP Altcourse and police officers. They analysed CCTV footage and records of mobile phone calls and looked into Cheshire Constabulary's policies and procedures. As a result of the investigation, both officers received written warnings.

In November 2007, an investigation was conducted by the Met's Directorate of Professional Standards and managed by the IPCC into the misuse of corporate American Express cards. The investigation was extensive as there were 3,530 card holders and all accounts were subject to review. A total of fifty-eight members of staff were subjected to criminal/disciplinary investigations, after which nine Met employees were charged with criminal offences and six convicted; eight officers were subject to misconduct hearings; twenty-four officers and staff were given written warnings, words of advice or management action; seventeen cases were assessed as requiring no further action.

To bring the subject of police corruption right up to date, at the time of writing this book, major allegations have been made by the *Daily Mail* against senior officers in the Metropolitan Police, in relation to Operation Midland. Operation Midland related to allegations involving sexual abuse and violence, made against high profile individuals, including the deceased former Government Minister Lord Leon Brittan. Carl Beech, who made the allegations of abuse, was given the pseudonym of 'Nick', and was later proven to have lied about these allegations. Indeed, Beech was later imprisoned for perverting the course of justice. Home Secretary Priti Patel ordered an independent review of the Met. The review was led by former High Court judge Sir Richard Henriques, and his report was published on 4 October 2019.

On 13 February 2021, the *Daily Mail* claimed that documents obtained by them under the Freedom of Information Act showed that, in the days prior to the Met's planned release of the un-redacted version of Sir Richard's report, Scotland Yard had launched an 'extraordinary spin operation' to ensure the Metropolitan Police Commissioner, Dame Cressida Dick, was not 'pulled into' the issues surrounding the controversial investigation. The article included copies of emails written by Cressida Dick and some of her senior colleagues, suggesting efforts were being made to protect the Commissioner.

On 2 October 2019, senior officers and the Met's media team were discussing what to issue to the Press alongside the report. The Deputy Commissioner, Sir Stephen House, asked Matt Horne, Head of Professional Standards, whether a scheduled call between the Commissioner and Sir Richard should now go ahead. 'My concern,' Sir Stephen wrote in an email, 'is that it is crucial that Cress [the Commissioner] is not pulled into this and a heated phone call may frustrate that imperative.' To add fuel to the fire, the *Mail* revealed that Matt Horne was appointed by the Met after being found guilty of misconduct in his former role as Deputy Chief Constable of Essex Police.

Other emails show the Met tried to gain support from the Mayor of London and the CPS. In one email to Mr Horne, he was asked whether Sadiq Khan or his deputy 'would be prepared to say publicly that they believe we have struck a good balance'.

The documents also showed that the police continued their investigations for three months after senior prosecutors suggested it should be abandoned. A summary of a December 2015 meeting between three Scotland Yard detectives and CPS lawyer Sally Walsh in London, and contained in a note that Sir Stephen was sent by Rebecca Lawrence, chief executive of the CPS, referred to the report of psychologist Bernice Andrews, an expert in historic child abuse, who had interviewed Carl Beech. The meeting summary said, 'We commenced by discussing the "elephant in the room", namely Professor Andrews' report to the effect that, in the absence of corroboration, "there must be serious doubt about the reliability of Nick's memories".'

*Dame Cressida Dick*

The note added, 'The police felt this was helpful in that it showed that we would be unable to rely on Nick's account alone in any prosecution but [name redacted] and Sally [Walsh] were clear that this report has fatally undermined the enquiry. We suggested that it should now be abandoned.'

Despite this, the investigation into the late Lord Brittan and former MP Harvey Proctor continued until the following March. Lord Bramall, a former D-Day hero, was cleared a month after police received the CPS's advice. Lady Brittan, whose homes were raided during Operation Midland, condemned a 'culture of cover-up' within the country's largest force, it was claimed by the *Daily Mail*.

Following the article, Sir Stephen House issued a statement claiming there had had been no cover-up. The Deputy Commissioner said, 'There have been calls for further inquiries or investigations to take place. However, Operation Midland is without doubt one of the most scrutinised investigations in policing history. There is no cover-up and nor has there been one. I want to say clearly that [the Met] is truly sorry for the harm caused by the mistakes made... and we fully understand why many of those people directly affected by the lies of Carl Beech and the investigation which followed remain deeply unhappy. The Commissioner and I have met Lord Bramall and Lady Brittan which has allowed us to apologise in person and to better understand how they feel. I want to reassure you that the lessons that have been learnt are being acted upon and that we are absolutely determined to keep making progress in implementing those lessons.'

The *Mail* revealed the next day that the Home Secretary was ordering another review by Her Majesty's Inspectorate of Constabulary. According to the report, Cressida Dick, in an email to senior officers and media advisers that day, described it as 'very irritating'. She insisted she welcomed an 'independent' review of the force but reiterated that officers could not be investigated again after they were cleared through the previous inquiry.

In a radio interview with LBC host Nick Ferrari, the Home Secretary, when questioned regarding Sir Richard Henriques's open letter calling for an independent investigation into Operation Midland, said, 'There are still questions. Rightly so, some have been put to me today, actually, very publicly in newspapers. The police are not above the law and there are many questions that still need looking at and investigating. I've seen the letter this morning and it is absolutely my responsibility to go back and look at some of these questions that are being posed.'

The second investigation, completed in March 2020, found that Scotland Yard's senior officers were more concerned with 'restricting access' to Sir Richard's report than learning lessons from it. It added that the Met had 'initially not done enough to learn the lessons from the Henriques report'. Those involved in Operation Midland, including former Deputy Assistant Commissioner Steve Rodhouse, are now facing calls from several quarters to explain why their investigation continued in the face of such damning advice.

This demonstrates yet again the extraordinary lengths some police officers, of whatever rank, will potentially go to, to lessen blame and paint things in a more favourable light! Whatever the rights and wrongs, this really doesn't look good and reflects poorly on some of the most senior police officers in the country.

The reality is that Operation Midland was flawed and poorly run, with far too much credibility given to Carl Beech whose allegations were totally uncorroborated. The oversight of the investigation, which was, for obvious reasons, very high-profile, was insufficient and for a detective superintendent to go public during an investigation, stating that allegations made were 'believable and credible', is something that should never have been allowed to happen.

The Met and the Commissioner should have been prepared to apologise unreservedly to the parties involved and their families. That way, they may have saved face. Allowing things to develop as they have undermines the credibility of both the individuals involved and the police service more generally in the eyes of the public. Only a full and independent investigation will now suffice.

I came across an article in *The Spectator* written by journalist Neil Darbyshire who also writes for the *Daily Mail*. Dated 2015, it is relatively recent. Referring to a report completed by the HMIC, he claimed that there had been three thousand reports of police corruption during the previous year and that only half had been properly investigated. He claimed that, for police officers in this country, corruption was becoming routine. He went on to accuse the police of increasingly using their powers to crack down not on criminals but on anyone who dared speak out against them. He believes that what was the finest, most honest service in the world was in danger of becoming rotten.

He cited a survey completed by 17,200 officers and staff who, he said, indicated that if they discovered corruption among their colleagues and chose to report it, they didn't believe their evidence would be treated in confidence and would fear 'adverse consequences'. He went on to claim that this appalling lack of protection for whistleblowers, often amounting to a form of persecution, had become commonplace throughout the public service and created a climate in which dishonesty and malpractice flourish.

He mentioned a second report, compiled by the then Serious Organised Crime Agency (now the NCA – National Crime Agency), which stated there had been a sharp increase over the past five years in the number of police officers dealing heroin, cocaine and amphetamines, and an equally startling rise in the number of officers abusing their power 'for sexual gratification', as mentioned earlier.

He moved on in his article to say that the suggested increase in cases of corruption and what he perceived as an apparent reluctance of police chiefs to combat it was 'a toxic combination'. As ever, he stated, Chief Constables blamed a lack of resources for not being able to pursue inquiries into claims of malpractice. He then accused the police of choosing to pursue ancient sex abuse allegations, and people who say unpleasant things on Twitter.

He acknowledged that the vast majority of Britain's police do a sometimes extremely arduous job with honesty, skill and good humour but, left unchecked, corruption could infect entire forces. He then referred to historic cases involving police corruption, several of which I have covered earlier in this book.

He made the point that he believed the police seemed to be retreating into a bunker of secrecy and paranoia where all news must be 'managed' and freedom of information is considered a threat. He pointed out that, on its website, the Metropolitan Police claimed to be committed to carrying out its duties with 'humility and transparency'. However, in his opinion, nothing could be further from the truth.

He described the history of past Met Police Commissioners, giving some support and praise for their methods. He stated that he felt that these men had respect for the office of constable, not least because they had all spent years on the front line before rising through the ranks. Further, they believed that part of their duty of accountability was to keep the public properly informed of what they were doing and why.

Interestingly, he then went on to say that he believed the present generation of police chiefs comes from quite a different breed. He believed them to have been fast-tracked and 'homogenised' from an early stage, so they can be difficult to tell apart. He said that they regularly used so-called management speak and accused them of self-interest regarding their own careers to the detriment of everything else. There are elements of this statement that I agree with. It is clear that Darbyshire reflected a vested interest in relation to what he described as the police pursuing journalists linked to the Leveson Inquiry. However, in saying this, he failed to point out that the whole investigation and the Leveson Inquiry were Government- rather than police-driven.

However, he did make a good point in the context of police corruption. He stated that all that he had described had wider implications for the integrity of the police. He stated that one of the consequences of heavy-handed police leadership, in order to pursue their own agenda, is that rank and file officers are encouraged to think they can do the same. Once ordinary officers start abusing power, a culture of semi-criminal behaviour becomes normal and whistleblowers are treated, not as honourable, but as traitors.

During the course of this book, one of the constant themes has been the issue of public confidence and the potential damage done to this when cases of police corruption are reported in the media. However, the only way to preserve and indeed improve public confidence in policing is to assist the public in making judgements about corrupt behaviour based on the context and to understand what constitutes serious corruption.

Therefore, public reporting of data related to police corruption and misconduct, as well as individual cases, is important to improve accountability and enhance public confidence. The current confusing array of definitions and ways of recording such allegations is unhelpful in achieving this. As well as providing consensus about whether particular types of cases constitute corruption, a single clear definition would allow answers to questions about how common it is, its key features, why it matters and whether it is a growing phenomenon.

The IPCC (now IOPC), in their report regarding corruption between 2008-2011, which I have previously mentioned, make the point that they intended to work with ACPO (now NPCC – National Police Chiefs Council), the CPS and other key interested parties to develop a shared definition of police corruption. Following this, they stated they would revise their guidance on the recording and referral of allegations, to ensure greater transparency and consistency for both the service and the public. Whilst the aim was to have completed this work by the end of 2012, as part of their plan to issue revised Statutory Guidance, I am not sure that this has been achieved in any meaningful way. There still seems to be a disparity across the police service in relation to these matters.

The IPCC reached the conclusion that information should be more routinely available to the public. The IPCC previously and now the IOPC already publish annual data on the public's complaints about the police and produce an annual report on deaths following police contact. The IOPC and police forces regularly release information on individual cases when these end in criminal or misconduct sanctions. At the same time, it should always be recognised that some matters must be kept confidential to protect current or future investigations. However, it is acknowledged, even to this day, that there is extraordinarily little in the public domain to show that actions are being taken against police corruption and the themes that have emerged from cases. Therefore, it should be a priority to provide regular updates on corruption investigations and key emerging themes, which should include information on why some behaviour, acceptable in other walks of life, is at best unacceptable and at worst corruption when conducted by a police officer or staff member.

The NPCC should be encouraged to consider taking similar action regarding anti-corruption work conducted across and within police forces. The objective of putting such information in the public domain would be to reassure the public that action is being taken to combat police corruption. Similarly, in the current structure, it should be ensured that the IOPC is exercising oversight or indeed dealing with the most serious cases themselves in order to re-assure the public that this area is being seriously addressed. This information should routinely be available to Police and Crime Commissioners (PCCs) to assist them in holding their Chief Constables to account on behalf of the public.

Current data as regards the recording and referral of corruption cases to the IOPC tends to show that these vary widely across police forces. These figures should not be seen as indicating which forces have a greater or lesser problem with corruption. It is more likely that they reflect differing local recording and/or referral practices across forces. Some forces may be taking a cautious approach and referring more corruption cases to the IOPC than they need to. Others, however, may not be referring to the IOPC the more serious cases that they must see. This was supported by the fact that a small number of forces had referred very few cases to the then IPCC over the three years that the report examined. From talking to those currently serving, this appears to still be the case now.

Chief Constables must ensure that their Professional Standards Departments refer cases to the IOPC when they meet the definition of serious corruption. Police forces should not wait to refer these cases to the IOPC until shortly before an arrest is to be made when, inevitably, they will have had little opportunity to provide effective oversight. Instead, a referral should be made when the likelihood of corrupt behaviour moves from the possible to the probable. In particular, forces should discuss referral with the IOPC in any case where they are making use of surveillance or other intrusive powers.

This change will inevitably result in higher levels of referral to the IOPC and they will undoubtedly argue that this will have potential resource implications. Nevertheless, most corruption allegations will still be dealt with by police forces themselves. That is the way the system is meant to work and I believe that current resources show that police forces themselves have significant resources, in the shape of Professional Standards Departments incorporating anti-corruption staffing, to deal with all but the most serious matters. However, there is understandably public concern, reflected in various surveys and reports in the media, about the police investigating themselves in this area. The IOPC has a statutory guardianship role over all complaints, whether or not they are investigated locally, and they should therefore be examining how best they can exercise that role. Part of that should include considering whether a more proactive approach is needed and can be resourced.

There is a clear understanding now that the public expects an independent body like the IOPC to investigate cases of serious police corruption. This is supported by previous reporting, which placed investigating police corruption as a higher priority for the IOPC than investigating deaths following police contact. Many of the cases involving so-called police contact are often tenuous as regards the level of that contact, to say the least. It is evident that, in most corruption cases, IOPC investigations can substantiate the need for misconduct proceedings, and in a large number of these, to uncover evidence that justifies a referral to the CPS relating to potential criminal conduct. There is, in my opinion, no doubt that the IOPC, in the absence of any other suitable organisation, should have oversight of the most serious cases of police corruption that cause greatest public concern and damage public confidence in policing. However, as I have mentioned previously, there is the potential for the HMIC&FRS to extend their current role to incorporate such work, thus keeping things under one roof. This should be considered, looking into the future.

Figures available show that there has been an increase in the number of independent investigations undertaken by the IOPC, relating to corruption matters. The IOPC now believes that it employs staff with the skills and experience to undertake investigations of overt corruption allegations. However, many within the police service doubt that this is the case. It will undoubtedly present a challenge for the IOPC to identify the resources required to undertake more of this work, while also conducting independent investigations into deaths following police contact, to ensure they can comply with their statutory duties. There is a need therefore to prioritise the apparently small number of the most serious allegations and, in particular, prioritise those matters involving senior officers, those involving gross abuse of powers for personal gain and others causing significant public concern. My personal concern is that any move for the IOPC to undertake large numbers of corruption investigations will inevitably lead to them requiring significant additional resources. There is a real risk that in times of financial restraint, this may come from the police budget or elsewhere from within the already hard-pressed public sector.

Therefore, it is not feasible for the IOPC to conduct covert independent investigations into corruption. This would require them to be a significantly different kind of organisation, with the considerable resources, specialist equipment, skills and staff time needed to undertake potentially long periods of surveillance. There are also practical issues, such as access to law enforcement agencies whose members are being investigated, and it is therefore unlikely that external IOPC investigators would be best placed to investigate cases of this type.

There is, however, always the option of using covert methods within overt independent cases and conducting covert independent investigations with specialist support, such as surveillance, from a law enforcement agency not connected to the case. If a case involves very senior officers, ie those of chief officer rank, then it is not easy for those with concerns about the behaviour of their superiors to know where to take them. Therefore, there must be an option for escalating such matters to an external body, whether HMIC&FRS, the NCA, or the IOPC. Therefore, the IOPC needs to work with those bodies, along with the CPS, to establish more effective systems that command public confidence.

Public confidence in, and acceptance of, police exercising their considerable powers over us all is heavily dependent on the public believing in the integrity of individual officers. That legitimacy is called into question and undermined by the kinds of behaviour described in cases such as those to which I have referred in this book or indeed by lesser examples of officers falling short of the standards of behaviour we expect. The public is rightly sceptical about the police service as a whole, when senior officers behave inappropriately, seem to claim 'there is no corruption here' or try to justify or minimise behaviour that the ordinary citizen sees as corrupt. This can include accepting generous hospitality, gaining personal benefit, or abusing their powers for personal gain. Public confidence is not enhanced by the fact that there is little public information about all of this. In fact, the opposite is true. The absence of reliable information, alongside press reporting of individual incidents, can fuel suspicion and distrust. The well-meaning claim made by the IPCC in their 2011 report regarding disclosure of this information has not been readily forthcoming, following the introduction of the IOPC.

Therefore, in summary, the following need to change.

There is a need for clearer information for the public on what constitutes police corruption. There must be regular analysis of corruption cases dealt with, identifying the emerging themes. There has to be a requirement for Chief Constables to ensure greater consistency in the recording and referral of corruption cases to the IOPC. This should be reinforced in the existing Statutory Guidance. A more effective national system for handling allegations against very senior officers ie those of chief officer rank, is essential. There is also a need to establish a more formalised and robust system for escalating such complaints.

Most corruption allegations will continue to be dealt with by the forces concerned, through their own Professional Standards and Anti-Corruption Units. However, in the current set up, the IOPC needs to consider how they can increase their involvement in the most serious cases of corruption.

The public expects serious corruption to be investigated by an organisation independent of the police. As already mentioned, the IOPC needs to be ready to take on more corruption cases, within existing resources if possible. Within those existing resources and in any event, the IOPC should continue to conduct a small, but increased, number of independent investigations into corruption cases, prioritising those involving senior officers, serious criminal allegations and gross abuse of police powers.

So, what are we talking about in terms of the numbers involved in such investigations within police forces? The number of people working in what the public will think of as *Line of Duty* roles to investigate complaints against officers, has soared in recent years. However, as an aside and as a former senior investigating officer responsible for investigating cases involving murder, I am deeply concerned that the numbers devoted to investigating murder, rape and organised crime gangs, have fallen.

With financial pressures hitting police budgets, the Professional Standards Departments have been identified as being one of the few areas that have expanded in recent years.

A Freedom of Information Act request made by a journalist contact of mine reveals that the numbers of officers and members of police staff (civilians) working in Professional Standards Departments have increased by fifteen percent in just the last two years.

Home Office figures show there were 1,034 officers and 1,150 civilians employed in the Professional Standards Departments of the nation's forces last year, compared to 917 officers and 978 civilians two years ago. The rise in police officers and staff tasked with investigating their colleagues comes as separate figures from the IOPC and shows that there were more than fifty-eight thousand internal police investigations last year.

Meanwhile, over the same two-year period, the number of police officers working in the Major Crime Units, investigating murders and rapes, fell from 2,614 to 2,493. Similarly, the last two years have seen a fall in the number of officers devoted to tackling cybercrime, with just 409 given that responsibility now, compared to 472 back in 2018.

The most recent IOPC statistics show that in the last five years, there has been a rise in sexual assault, corruption and unfairness cases, as well as discrimination allegations levelled at police officers and staff. In that five-year time span, the number of sex assault cases levelled against police officers has risen from 110 to last year's tally of 143, while corruption or malpractice allegations rose from 577 to 624. Across the same time period, the number of cases where officers were accused of discriminatory behaviour jumped from 1,422 to 1,580.

Figures relating to the number of officers and police (civilian) staff working in the Professional Standards Departments of Police Forces in England and Wales for the period since 2012 are as follows:

2012: 1,394
2013: 1,406
2014: 1,465
2015: 1,564
2016: 1,731
2017: 1,878
2018:1,895
2019: 2,069
2020: 2,184

On the back of these figures, there seem to be plenty of officers and staff devoted to investigating misconduct allegations. Indeed, if we then add on what resources are available to the IOPC, the numbers involved are considerable and could rightly be seen as very high, compared with other areas of policing.

However, what price public confidence?

There is a view that the police can never be successful in fighting crime if they are obliged to operate within the rules. In the book *Bent Coppers* by James Morton, there is a quote attributed to Edward Clarke QC who represented officers in the Brighton corruption case previously referred to, who stated, 'You do not... if you are trying to catch them, follow the Queensbury Rules. You use what methods you can for the purpose of getting the people arrested and punished'.

So, we end where we began. The public expect the police to catch criminals and the majority are probably not that bothered about how this is achieved, at least in the first instance. However, when things go wrong and police corruption becomes the issue, public confidence, as we know, is damaged.

Therefore, a balance is needed. However, the problem with allowing controlled deviance to fight crime ie bent on behalf of the public, is that it becomes that much easier to accept, and more difficult to control, individual deviance, ie bent for oneself. In the same book just referred to, Tony Judge, a previous editor of *Police Review*, is quoted as saying, 'I believe the public has lost its sense of innocence about the police without understanding why. So it is no longer shocked at the revelation of police malpractice as it used to be. There is an unspoken understanding on what they can do but they can use legal and extra-legal means to keep the lid on. The more legislation, the more the allegations of malpractice. You will end up with a very clean police force but a very ineffective crime fighting force.'

Perhaps this is now where we are. Currently available statistics at least show that the ability of the police to clear up crime has never been as low.

I will leave the final words with CH Rolph, another contributor to *Police Review*. He stated in *Bent Coppers*, 'You ask me how deviance can be contained? I don't think it can. It's universal and endemic. It invades every level of administration and government in every country. If ever "social ethics" became an educational subject which had a firmer base than mythological religions, which themselves eat away at the community importance of truth, I mean simply telling the truth, the chances would begin to improve. As it is, lying is an essential instrument of "law and order".'

That final quote perhaps demonstrates the fact that corruption and misconduct will always exist, whether within the police or elsewhere. Ultimately, it is we, the public, who need to decide what it is that we want, and what we are prepared to accept, in terms of policing.

# BIBLIOGRAPHY

http://www.policecrimes.co.uk/

https://www.bing.com/search?q=police+corruption+and+misconduct+cases&form=ANNTH1&refig=77389dbc255b4876b2d286630d70700c&sp=1&qs=RI&pq=police+misconduct+and+corruption&sk=PRES1&sc=3-32&cvid=77389dbc255b4876b2d286630d70700c

https://www.oldpolicecellsmuseum.org.uk/content/history/police_history/bent-cops

https://www.oldpolicecellsmuseum.org.uk/content/history/police_history/the_brighton_police_corruption_casehttps://www.independent.co.uk/news/west-midlands-serious-crime-squad-police-unit-to-blame-for-dozens-more-injustices-1120219.html

https://assets.publishing.service.gov.uk/government/uploads/system/uploads/attachment_data/file/287030/stephen_lawrence_review_summary.pdf

https://policeconduct.gov.uk/news/stephen-lawrence-corruption-investigation-enters-new-phase

https://www.theguardian.com/uk-news/2019/jul/02/stephen-lawrence-ex-detective-cleared-of-corruption

https://www.theguardian.com/uk-news/2018/apr/19/corrupt-met-officers-protected-family-of-stephen-lawrence-murderer

https://www.bbc.co.uk/news/uk-26474458

https://hydeparknow.uk/2015/08/14/the-met-polices-attack-on-five-holloway-boys-a-horrific-1980s-crime-investigated/

*Ugly Bus*. Mike Thomas, 2014

https://www.itv.com/news/wales/story/2012-11-22/no-charges-for-cardiff-three-officer/

http://tonymusings.blogspot.com/2010/12/1987-trial-and-its-aftermath.html

https://www.independent.co.uk/news/uk/crime/west-yorkshire-police-conspiracy-fit-up-burglars-elizabeth-belton-judith-mulligan-a8746691.html

https://www.walesonline.co.uk/news/wales-news/swansea-sex-shop-murder-latest-2075370

https://www.dailymail.co.uk/news/article-2732033/Almost-100-police-officers-year-suspended-alleged-corruption.html

https://assets.publishing.service.gov.uk/government/uploads/system/uploads/attachment_data/file/243479/9780108511622.pdf

https://www.justiceinspectorates.gov.uk/hmicfrs/wp-content/uploads/pic-literature-review.pdf

https://www.justiceinspectorates.gov.uk/hmicfrs/media/police-integrity-19990601.pdf

https://api.parliament.uk/historic-hansard/commons/1986/nov/04/detective-superintendent-lundy

https://www.oldpolicecellsmuseum.org.uk/content/history/police_history/how-policing-started-in-england

http://eprints.bournemouth.ac.uk/783/1/Kiely_Output_1.pdf

https://www.phrases.org.uk/meanings/canteen-culture.html

https://www.tutor2u.net/sociology/topics/canteen-culture

https://www.jstor.org/stable/23637974?seq=1

https://www.app.college.police.uk/app-content/covert-policing/undercover-policing/

https://www.college.police.uk/News/College-news/Pages/undercover-policing-guide.aspx

https://www.ucpi.org.uk/?cookie-state-change=1594133606512

https://www.mirror.co.uk/news/uk-news/police-across-uk-pay-undercover-21387925

https://news.sky.com/story/police-informants-where-should-line-be-drawn-10980924

https://www.bbc.co.uk/news/uk-38902480

https://www.theguardian.com/uk/2009/apr/25/police-surveillance-sources-informants

https://policinginsight.com/features/analysis/police-forces-must-take-a-firm-and-unified-stance-on-tackling-sexual-abuse-of-position/

*Lundy*. Martin Short, 1992

*Bent Coppers*. James Morton, 1993

*Talking Blues*. Roger Graef, 1989

Error of Judgement – The Truth About The Birmingham Bombings. Chris Mullin, 1986

*Scotland Yard's Cocaine Connection*. Andrew Jennings et al, 1991

https://www.spectator.co.uk/article/the-shocking-truth-about-police-corruption-in-britain

https://www.justiceinspectorates.gov.uk/hmicfrs/wp-content/uploads/police-integrity-and-corruption-2015.pdf

The Hillsborough Independent Panel Report. September 2012

*Police (Canteen) Sub-Culture: An Appreciation*. PA J Waddington The British Journal of Criminology Vol 39, No 2 (Spring 1999), pp 287-309

*The Politics Of The Police*. Robert Reiner, 2010

The Police Occupational Culture In Anglo-American Societies. Manning P, 1995

Corruption In The Police Service Of England And Wales. IPCC report of 2011

# ACKNOWLEDGEMENTS

I wish to begin by thanking my publisher, Penny Reeves of Saron Publishers, for her time, patience, sound professional advice and understanding once again in helping me to write and then publish this book.

Very special thanks go to my family and especially my wife Ann. She has been with me right throughout my journey as a police officer from beginning to end. Without her, most of my achievements would not have been possible.

I also wish to thank my many friends and colleagues for their unwavering support and friendship over the period of my long career. There are simply too many to list the names of here. However, you will all know who you are. Without you, what I have achieved over the years would not have been possible. Policing, perhaps more than any other profession, relies on the men and women who serve within it for their dedication, teamwork, courage and public spiritedness. It has been my privilege to have worked with some of the very best in this regard.

Whilst this book is about police misconduct and corruption, it needs to be remembered that the vast majority of police officers are highly professional, decent and honest individuals, undertaking what is a very difficult job and doing it well.

Police officers are ordinary human beings and are therefore susceptible to the same failings as anyone else. Just because they are police officers doesn't make them immune to temptation and bad behaviour. However, I believe that most who choose to take on the role are indeed very special people. But then I am biased, of course!

# ABOUT THE AUTHOR

*Kevin Moore with his first book My Way*

Kevin Moore joined Sussex Police at the age of twenty-one years in June 1978. After joining the police, the author spent his two-year probationary period at Brighton during which time he operated as a beat officer and area car driver/observer. Whilst there, he experienced a wide variety of policing situations as one would expect in terms of the cosmopolitan nature of a City the size of Brighton and Hove. Following this, he became a rural beat patrol officer at Camber near Rye in East Sussex.

A short while later, he entered the Criminal Investigation Department (CID) as a detective constable. This proved to be the start of a long and productive career as a detective during which time he climbed the ranks, ultimately achieving the highest rank possible in the CID world of Detective Chief Superintendent when he was the Head of Sussex's CID. During his service, he was the senior detective in charge of the CID at Hastings and Eastbourne. He also worked within the Professional Standards Department investigation complaints made against police officers.

He served as the Chief Superintendent and Divisional Commander of Brighton and Hove during which time he was responsible for all police operations in the City as well as working with key partner agencies including the City's Council. He took command of many large-scale public order demonstrations as well as other major public safety events.

During his detective career, he was a Senior Investigating Officer (SIO) with a responsibility for leading enquiries into homicide and other major crime investigations. He was viewed as being a highly competent senior detective. He was formerly a member of the International Homicide Investigators Association.

Following his retirement as a police officer in 2009, after more than thirty-one years of service, he took up a position with the newly formed SE Regional Organised Crime Unit as a civilian member of staff. This involved the role of Regional Intelligence Manager and then subsequently that of the SE Regional Prison Intelligence Manager. This Unit has an overall responsibility for investigating the criminal activities of those involved in the commission of the most serious types of crime.

He fully retired from the police service in January 2018. He has been married to Ann for over forty-three years and they have two grown up children and five grandchildren. He holds a BA (Hons) Degree in Public Sector and Police Studies and a Post Graduate Diploma in Police Studies. He is interested in football and cricket, having previously been a player, coach and administrator. He now spends much of his time with his wife, her Golden Retriever dogs and their three horses.

He continues to support the Police Service and is prepared to articulate his dismay at the consequences the severe budget cuts have had on the spirit within the ranks and the level of competency of leadership, whilst acknowledging the remarkable work officers carry out daily. To help ensure that those responsible for the running of the Police Service are held to account and are challenged when required, he created a group called Retired Police Officers Who Care.

He is the current secretary of his local Eastbourne and District NARPO (National Association of Retired Police Officers) Branch. Kevin also carries out media work regarding police-related topics which includes TV, Radio and newspapers, as well as film documentaries.

This is Kevin's third book following on from *My Way* and *Real Murder Investigations*.

# ABOUT THE PUBLISHERS

Saron Publishers has been in existence since 2005, producing niche magazines. Our first venture into books took place in 2016 when we published *The Meanderings of Bing* by Tim Harnden-Taylor. The third offering from Bing, *The Ruminations of Bing,* was published in July 2019. *Minstrel Magic* by Eleanor Pritchard came out in 2017 and tells the phenomenal show business story of the George Mitchell Singers and the Black and White Minstrels. Further publications planned for 2021 include *Newport Operatic Society – The First One Hundred Years* by David Kenny, and *The Best of Times* by Eugene Barter.

Email info@saronpublishers.co.uk to join our mailing list. We promise no spam.

Visit our website saronpublishers.co.uk to keep up to date and to read reviews of what we've been reading and enjoying.

Follow us on Facebook @saronpublishers.

Follow us on Twitter @saronpublishers.

Printed in Great Britain
by Amazon

63271267R00139